COOPERATION ▪ COMMITMENT **WATERSHED** COURAGE ▪ CAUTION ▪ CARING

Watershed: A Successful Voyage Into Integrative Learning

Mark Springer

NATIONAL MIDDLE SCHOOL ASSOCIATION

NMSA

Mark Springer has taught at Radnor Middle School in Wayne, Pennsylvania, for twenty years, the last seven as co-director of the award-winning Watershed program. He has also taught at the high school and college levels.

The National Middle School Association is grateful to Mark for his pioneering work in whole learning and for preparing this particularly timely volume. Appreciation is also expressed to Mary Mitchell, who designed the book and prepared it for printing and to Barbara Brannon for her original art work on the cover.

Contents

Acknowledgements

As the record of an educational odyssey, this book about the WATER-SHED Program has been a journey in its own right. Since setting out originally seven years ago, I have explored numerous highways and byways trying to find and to chart an appropriate route which others could follow into the realms of integrative studies. Always challenging, the journey often proved arduous and frustrating. Many times I lost my way. Fortunately, each time I reached a crossroads of doubt or indecision, I found friends to encourage me or to point me once again in the right direction. To these many friends I owe enduring gratitude. I would like, in some small way, to acknowledge my debt by dedicating this book to these people:

First and foremost to my wife, Allison, and to my children, Colin and Lauren, who have sacrificed more than anyone else for the sake of WATERSHED; to Ed Silcox and Woody Arnold, my constant companions on this journey, whose ideas and enthusiasm constitute the very heart and soul of WATERSHED; to our earliest mentors, most notably to Bob Struble at the Brandywine Valley Association, our first principal, Anne Janson, school board members Jane Beatty and Ruth Payne, and our superintendent Dr. John DeFlaminis without whose support the journey would never have been possible; and to my newer friend, John Lounsbury of the National Middle School Association, who first read this manuscript and promoted its publication.

Finally, I wish to thank each and every one of the WATERSHED students and their parents. It is, after all, their commitment and courage which make the program work and make the continuing journey worthwhile.

July, 1994   Mark Springer

Foreword

Some men see things as they are, and ask, "Why?" Other men dream things that never were, and ask, "Why not?"

This idea of George Bernard Shaw's, paraphrased and popularized by Senator Robert F. Kennedy, came to mind as I first read the *Watershed* manuscript. Given an opportunity, Mark Springer and Ed Silcox, experienced teachers, said, "Why not?"—as much with an exclamation point as a question mark. Thus began an educational odyssey of true significance.

Through these pages walk with Mark and Ed as they turn dream into reality, developing a full day experiential program for forty seventh graders in a public school. Via an engaging narrative, author Mark Springer chronicles this adventure in teaching and learning, giving ample detail to the program's initiation, its difficulties, its triumphs. Freed from the traditional organizational barriers of subjects and schedules which often make education artificial and irrelevant, these courageous pioneers created a whole learning program that involves students in real life activities, leads them to become responsible for their own education, and integrates all learning.

The *Watershed* story is a remarkable and often touching chronology. It is inspirational as well as informative, honest and reality-based. The narrative is sprinkled with interesting bits of Americana, the culture of the Native Americans who inhabited eastern Pennsylvania, and mini-lessons from American history. This book is an also unabashed testimony for whole learning. The author doesn't hide his disappointment that comparable whole learning programs haven't materialized at his school and only three such projects are to be initiated elsewhere this fall.

Student drawings and photographs not only increase the book's attractiveness but give it a sense of reality. The ample appendices provide copies of pertinent documents, student projects, record keeping forms, and research topics actually used at various times in the program's first six years.

Watershed will excite and inspire you—and perhaps you may be challenged to conclude, "Why not?"

—John H. Lounsbury

"You Boys Didn't Really Think You Were Going to Get Away With This, Did You?"

I'd like to think that the water swirling softly around our shins knew and cared that we were there—a ring of us, 40 seventh graders, Ed and me standing mid-stream just below the Route 842 bridge. It's always tempting to think of the Brandywine as a living friend, glad to see us when we arrive, somehow different when we leave. We've come to know this river and its neighboring streams so well; and, like the process of education itself, rivers are custom made for allegories.

The autumnal equinox glistened. High overhead we spotted first one, then two, and eventually more than twenty turkey vultures spiraling easily in the late September sunshine reflecting our circle below in the current. As if on cue, a solitary osprey appeared upstream gliding swiftly toward us along currents only it could sense. Gracefully, effortlessly, the osprey arched eastward over the field of stinging nettles, assuring itself that we had not disturbed its domain during our short trek from the road to the river. The osprey could not know what pains these kids, duly warned of tingling terrors, had taken to avoid contact with any and all plants along the narrow path from bus to bank. Satisfied of our honorable intentions, the regal bird gave us one last glance before it drifted silently toward the forks and vanished.

Standing there in the riffles, I, too, felt a certain sense of rightness as I thought back over the events that had brought us here, both to this particular spot, and to this inauguration of a new approach to public education, a "whole learning" approach we call WATERSHED. Ed and I, like the Brandywine's two branches, had reached this juncture near the forks from similar yet separate directions. We, too, had traveled meandering paths to meet here and begin this journey together with these students. Ed arrived by way of the environmental sciences; I through a more circuitous route of literature, history, and the arts. Yet, here we were, welcoming each student in turn to this special place, the Brandywine River, and to this special program, WATERSHED.

There is much debate concerning the Brandywine's sources. So many first order streams filament the Welsh Hills of northwestern Chester County, Pennsylvania, that it is virtually impossible, certainly impractical, to say which is the "true" source of each branch. Wilmer W. MacElree, in his 1906 edition of *Down the Eastern and Up the Black Brandywine,* claims that both branches seep up within one half mile of each other just northeast of the farming community of Honeybrook. United States Geological Survey topographical maps clearly substantiate that possibility, and our personal observations, clouded though they may be by romanticism, lend additional credence to MacElree's theory. I remember the magical awe I felt when I first saw the twin streams, neither of which is a good pace wide, winding through a cow pasture. I had set out purposefully to find them, else it's doubtful I ever would have noticed them. I was, however, well guided by MacElree's 80 year old volume, a ten year old road map of Chester County, and my nine year old son who navigated and valiantly tried to record my periodic observations and calculations. I don't think he understood my excitement as we played tag with the shrinking stream along narrow roads winding among corn fields and cow pastures.

I don't think he understood the enthusiasm with which I stopped the car as we crossed a damp ditch that I believe to be the most likely source of the west branch. Fortunately for us both, we had our seat belts securely fastened and no other cars happened by. Finding the birthplace of a stream, actually watching it be reborn with each drop of water welling up from the seep, is truly a magical experience. My son was not impressed, but I'll never forget that moment.

Nor will I forget a similar moment several months later when I traversed the spot again. This time I asked the bus driver to stop so all forty-two of us, students and teachers alike, could stare with simultaneous disbelief and wonder at the infant river.

So, I accept without debate the twin sources MacElree described: you can make up your own mind. There can be no doubt, however, that the Brandywine River, nee "Creek," springs from the lush and fertile heights of those hills named for the Welsh Quakers who settled there some three hundred years ago.

Similarly, though we could debate *ad nauseum* the metaphysical beginnings of our journey to this point, I know, and I believe Ed would concur, that WATERSHED is the natural point toward which our respective training and careers, again like the river, had inevitably been flowing. For those among you less willing or able to accept this organic view, I'm willing to put aside Zen, kismet, and serendipity, and to allow that the journey began in earnest several years before when Ed and I tied his red canoe atop my blue station wagon, squeezed six kids in the back, and set out in search of fossils along the Chesapeake-Delaware Canal.

As part of our school's High Potential Program for academically gifted students, a program which Ed and I co-managed at that time, we created a series of special field trips. We called these outings Academic Excursions: "excursions" because we were taking the students out of school into the larger world; "academic" because the students earned their seat on a trip by completing research on a related topic before we would arrange an appropriate trip. Often their research determined the type of trip or the destination arranged. Such an Academic Excursion was our fossil hunting trip to areas along the Chesapeake-Delaware Canal, areas that were more accessible from a canoe than from a car. That trip led to many other stream related excursions and to the conviction that canoes, rivers, and kids go naturally together.

...rivers and kids go naturally together .

The success of these trips and the enthusiasm with which the students reacted to them subsequently led us to build two wood strip canoes with our students, and our fates were sealed. By the time we acquired five canoes, it was apparent that all kids, not just the "gifted" students with whom we had been working, could benefit from the experience of discovering a river first-hand.

It was also clear to us that we needed a trailer. So, we set out to find a suitable trailer and, in our travels, found a program as well. Being relatively good teachers who try to practice what we preach, Ed and I did our homework. We scoured magazines, newspapers, and telephone books in search of references to canoe trailers. We knew they existed: we had seen them frequently on our travels near rivers. These trailers look like twin, albeit abbreviated telephone poles stuck on wheels, and they generally held six or eight stacked canoes. Yet our searches proved futile and our inquiries continuously yielded the same conclusion: we would have to build one of our own. Thus we decided to purchase a regular sixteen foot boat trailer and convert it to suit our needs. We located a good buy, obtained the necessary financial approval from our district administration, and set out one September morning in 1985 for Brick, New Jersey, to pick up our trailer. The day was a religious holiday, so school was not in session. To pass the time on the two hour drive we discussed numerous ideas, options, and permutations for an alternative program that might offer all types of students the advantages we had seen in "gifted" education. We dreamed aloud of a program that would break down the barriers and cubbyholes created by the bureaucracies inherent in traditional educational systems. We wanted the students to experience their learning first-hand in a real world way, rather than through the sterilizing screen of conventional curricula neatly rolled into forty-five minute segments like TV sitcoms. We debated grade levels, time frames, approaches, and final products as we drove through the Jersey pinelands; our dialogue frequently punctuated by sightings of turkey vultures and red-tailed hawks. By the time we reached the distributor, we had narrowed our focus: *watersheds!*

We wanted the students to experience their learning first hand in a real-world way.

It took another two hours to put the paper work and the lighting connections together. Fortunately, the dealer—a canoe enthusiast himself—willingly lent us a portable hitch. Novices that we were, thoughts of hitches had never crossed our minds .

Nor, for that matter, had the notion of a license.

Ten miles down the road, flashing red lights in the rear view mirror signaled the beginning of an ordeal that lasted the next five hours, cost us ninety dollars, and convinced us once and for all that radical changes were needed. The young officer asked for the trailer's papers which Ed produced with naive assurance. "Where's the registration?" the officer inquired as he thumbed methodically through the packet we had been given by the dealer.

"The dealer told us everything we needed was there," Ed explained politely. "The trailer is being registered by a school district in Pennsylvania. That's where we're headed now."

This evidently proved too much for the officer to handle on his own. So, he bid us wait in our vehicle, parked conspicuously on the wide, sandy, unshaded shoulder while he returned to his patrol car to radio his superiors for advice. The sun, augmented by those flashing red lights, grew very hot over the next fifteen minutes.

"I'm sorry, men, but you'll have to unhitch the trailer. We'll have it taken to a compound until you get proper papers. Tow truck is on its way."

"But . . ."

"Sorry; and may I have your driver's license again? I'm going to have to issue you a citation."

"But . . ."

Ten minutes later, the flatbed truck arrived. A monstrous driver descended from the cab and greeted the officer. Obviously they knew each other. Cable, hook, winch, the dastardly deed was accomplished quickly. As we waved good-bye to our brand new trailer, I began to suspect that these men had done this sort of thing before.

Now I'm sure New Jerseyites love their Department of Motor Vehicles. Being from Pennsylvania, however, we had no experience with this bureaucratic paradise. Thus, it came as somewhat of a surprise when, after a lengthy search, we finally found the local DMV branch office cleverly camouflaged as a storefront in a small shopping center. So well was it concealed that at first I honestly thought it was a laundromat. Now that I think about it, maybe it was. I certainly felt like I had been taken to the cleaners, put through the wringer, and hung out to dry by the time we finally re-emerged from the sterilizing fluorescence into the waning sunshine some two hours later.

Were I Dante, I now would have a whole new perspective from which to describe purgatory: powder blue, speckled, linoleum tile floors reeking of antiseptic cleanser, faded darker blue walls lined with chrome, straight-back chairs—the kind with the blue molded plastic seats—each occupied by a formless, blank-faced mass. A dismal array of shoes tapped a cacophony of bored blues rhythms which echoed endlessly off the blue walls and floor. Five teller-type windows yawned along the far wall. From each extended a dreary line of weary souls waiting their turn to feed the monster machine beyond the wall. Teletypes and typewriters clicked and clacked ominously as the creature gnashed its teeth. At each orifice a colorless clerk routinely processed routine papers without expression or comment. We selected a line and waited. After what seemed an eternity, we finally reached the window. We explained our situation: we needed a temporary trailer license to get our new trailer out of detention, out of New Jersey, and back to Pennsylvania. The clerk stared at us without expression.

"Please move to the next window; I don't handle that."

"But . . ."

"Next!" We shuffled to the back of the line stretching from the next window.

We waited . . .

and we waited . . .

Another clerk . . .

Same story . . .

Another robotic rejection . . . another line . . . another window.

We started to laugh. What else could any sane soul do under these insane circumstances? We laughed so loud that I worried another officer would be called to arrest us for disorderly conduct. I shouldn't have worried; no one seemed to notice us at all. We finally made contact with a young lady who took pity on us, pulled strings, charged us five bucks, and handed us a "temporary license." I suspect we may have brightened her day. The license later proved a worthless invention on her part, but it worked. Makes one wonder, doesn't it?

Armed with this "legal" paperwork, we set out to rescue our trailer. The garage, an ominously plain cinder block fortress surrounded by a chain-link and barbed-wire fence, was well guarded. The cyclopean tow-truck operator stood silently in the back, dimly lit corner of the tiny dungeon-like office beyond an iron-barred window. At that window an ancient dame, her cigarette ash lengthening and drooping as she talked, inspected our new "license."

"That'll be sixty dollars," she wheezed at last.

I choked.

"Do you take credit cards?" Ed inquired politely, and we each reached for our wallets.

The driver edged threateningly closer to the bars.

"Cash," she wheezed again as the ash from her cigarette fell to the counter.

"May I write you a check?"

"Cash," she repeated without emotion.

The driver took another step forward, his teeth shining in the semi-darkness. I thought I heard him snarl.

Fortunately, between us Ed and I had exactly $61.25. The giant grunted as the lady took our money. I think he was disappointed. Then he slouched toward an unseen back door to free our captive trailer.

As we turned to exit, the old woman cackled, "I've just got one question…"

We turned to face her again.

She exhaled a big cloud of blue smoke. "You boys didn't really think you were going to get away with this, did you?"

Two years later, almost to the day, Ed and I stood in the Brandywine River surrounded by eager seventh graders, and the question came back to me. As I watched the turkey vultures spiral lazily above us, and I thought back over the journey that had brought us here—the problems, the criticisms, the questions we had faced; the victories, and the support we had found—I felt again that sense of rightness.

I looked at the smiling faces surrounding me. Here were students who wanted to learn; who were excited about being "in school," about being in WATERSHED.

"Get away with this?"

I chuckled inwardly.

Since that September morning in the Brandywine, we have enjoyed seven WATERSHED years. We have explored other rivers and creeks, tried new ideas, and shared the thrill of true learning along with more than two hundred and fifty seventh graders. WATERSHED, now so much more than a wild idea hatched on an insane day, continues to prosper and grow. It represents the fulfillment of a personal dream and the seed of a much larger vision of what education in America could become.

WATERSHED represents the fulfillment of a personal dream and the seed of a much larger vision of what education in America could become.

It is toward that very vision that this book is directed. By sharing the WATERSHED story, we want to encourage others to try similar projects, to push the boundaries of education beyond the confines of traditional curricula and conventional formats. We would like this book to convince administrators, teachers, and parents that education can succeed in more dynamic, more natural forms well beyond even those somewhat lessened restrictions found in so-called "interdisciplinary learning" strategies. We would like this book to point toward the emergence of a workable educational system truly based on whole learning; an educational system based as well on the belief that every student deserves to feel a sense of ownership, a sense of pride, and a sense of belonging. If nothing else, the WATERSHED story is a testament to the feasibility of that grander vision; a vision which can be fulfilled if we all have the courage to put our knowledge and convictions into action.

True to that goal, and to the WATERSHED methodology as well, this will not be a typical textbook. Those of you looking for a pre-packaged "How-To" handbook have already missed the point and will likely be both disappointed and bewildered by what follows. Those of you searching for classroom-ready ideas will find many specific activities described, but you will not find an entire prescribed curriculum ready for packaged use. Those of you seeking the comforting support of footnoted studies written in pseudo-scientific jargon by educational authorities will be similarly disappointed. Such evidence exists and can be readily found by any interested reader, but it has no place in this particular book. A limited bibliography of such sources is provided, however, in Appendix H.

This book simply conveys the history and the development of a workable whole learning program through a series of interrelated, often allegorical, experiences and observations. Successes and failures alike have been duly noted, along with problems confronted and solutions attempted. Along the way, the reader will catch a glimpse of some of the content we happen to cover as well.

Thus, in a very real sense, this is a working document. Even as I have been writing, both the book and the program have been changing and evolving. By definition, no whole learning program can be pinned down to a textbook approach. Yet, I believe that when the WATERSHED story is viewed as a whole, and if its lessons are applied, this constitutes a working theory and practice for whole learning.

"Get away with this?"

It is out of our hands. This story belongs to all the WATERSHED students over the years who had the courage to take a chance, who cared enough to nurture a dream, and who had the commitment to prove that visions can become a reality. What is more, it is about to belong to you, which puts that responsibility on you as well.

"Get away with this?"

I think so. **ɰ**

"Nature's Classroom" by Erika Bausman, 1994

Beginnings

1.

If this story has a beginning, then WATERSHED officially began some two weeks or so before our ill-fated trip to New Jersey. At that time, as the 1985 school year opened, the school district administrators announced a new approach to the time-honored traditions of staff in-service days. For those of you who may not be part of the teaching profession, In-service days are those often boring days teachers spend struggling to remain attentive to professional guest experts spouting motivational mumbo-jumbo or recycling stale ideas from Education 101 in glossy new jargon or packaging. One would think that after these tastes of their own medicine, most teachers would jump at the chance to change their teaching techniques.

At any rate, tiring of the teachers' complaints about these days wasted sitting through inane sessions, the administrators said, "Fine, you think you can do better? Prove it. Instead of the usual in-service days, each teacher will design a personal development plan to utilize the scheduled in-service time effectively. Plans will be submitted for the approval of building principals by September . . ."

"Just don't throw me into that briar patch!"

The plans submitted, as one might expect, varied greatly. They ranged from taking bona fide graduate courses in classroom management to visiting the Poconos (with the wife and kids, of course) to "check out the geomorphology of the Appalachian Range."

Ed and I had been musing for years about ideal curricula, problems in public education, and other related issues. In fact, we discussed such issues almost constantly in our planning for the gifted program which we had developed and directed together since 1980. All our discussions, as stimulating as they were, inevitably ended in the same frustrated admission: "Well, that would be great, but where would we find the time to work out all the details?" Now we were being given that time, so we decided to use the required in-service days to see what we could create.

Certain givens existed as far as we were concerned. First and foremost, the program had to be open to all students. We had long since wearied of the artificial distinctions created to divide students into groups; distinctions which too frequently held students back rather than helping them to progress. I could cite numerous examples of this from our work in the gifted program, but one in particular comes immediately to mind. Because of the "revolving door" format of our gifted program, we could work with individual students for varying lengths of time on student initiated projects. Often teachers recommended students to us for special work, and we would plan projects with these students whether they were identified as being gifted or not. We were working under these circumstances with one young girl when state program auditors happened to pay us a surprise visit. When they checked our records and discovered that this young lady was not among the population identified as gifted, we were reprimanded, and the child's work was brought to an immediate stop. Shortly thereafter, at our request, the young lady was tested and found to have an I.Q. far above the required level. In fact, she had one of the highest I.Q. scores we had ever seen. Suddenly we were allowed to work with her again. Clearly the child had not changed; she was gifted whether the state recognized it or not. Only the bureaucratic distinctions and procedures had kept her from working with us. Too often, based on these faulty distinctions and procedures, only the *identified* gifted or learning disabled students reap the benefits of unique or individualized programming. We maintain that all students are gifted in some ways and disabled in others: all deserve more individualized attention. Thus, we wanted to work with a heterogeneous grouping of students from all ability levels. Furthermore, we wanted to prove that all students, regardless of so-called ability levels, can work together effectively and can benefit from their shared experience .

...the program had to be open to all students.

In addition, the curriculum had to go beyond the traditional disciplines, and even beyond the prevalent definition of interdisciplinary studies. We wanted a program based on whole learning—the total reintegration of knowledge. Both of us have devoted our careers to breaking down the artificial walls of academia; the walls that divide students, and the walls that divide knowledge. We had long believed that learning does not come neatly packaged in forty-five minute lessons. Nor does learning confine itself to the blocks and titles we educators assign it. Indeed, the answers to a problem in one so-called subject area often surface more readily when viewed from the perspective of some other so-called subject area. Every

We wanted a program based on whole learning.

good teacher knows this is true; as do scientists, business executives, artists, and just about everyone faced with a real life problem. Why, then, should we impose an unreal, artificial structure on an all too real process?

I know some argue that the need for expertise and in-depth control of minutiae requires this divisive emphasis on separated disciplines. After all, these same voices contend, you would want your surgeon to be an expert carefully trained and detail oriented, wouldn't you? Of course I would. However, in the first place, one cannot assume that the implementation of curricula based on separate disciplines ensures that type of learning. After all, separate disciplines constitute the very type of curriculum American education has employed for the last one hundred years; the self-same type of curriculum so continually under fire these days for producing falling SAT scores and increasing numbers of illiterate graduates each year. And that's not to mention the numbers of frustrated drop-outs this method produces.

Furthermore, one should not assume that an interdisciplinary or whole learning approach precludes the mastering of specifics. When correctly implemented, these programs can lead to greater understanding and retention of specific details. The whole learning approach provides more contexts and connections for facts and thus more avenues for their retrieval and application in different situations. Facts and concepts are mastered without relying on out-dated, boring methods involving rote memorization. They are mastered instead through continual application in meaningful contexts.

Finally, there is a great difference between a surgeon and a seventh grader. Plenty of time is available in college and graduate school for those who so desire to receive training in a specific discipline. Seventh graders need to see a bigger picture. They need a larger framework of background relationships and experiences into which they can later slip the pertinent details of any chosen career. This becomes vitally important as we note that most of today's students will be likely to change careers several times in the future. How to learn and the desire to learn must take precedence over the particulars of a limited disciplinary study. Ironically, it is just that desire to learn, that joy of discovery which many traditional curricula and conventional school structures tend to destroy rather than promote.

How to learn and the desire to learn must take precedence.

Furthermore, now that I think of it, I also hope that hypothetical surgeon of mine will be able to see me as a whole person and not just as a textbook schematic of specific veins, arteries, and sundry organs!

Grades had to go.

Our third given: grades had to go. Our own personal school experiences as students as well as our experiences in gifted education reinforced our belief that grades are truly arbitrary and counter-productive. Grades imply some universal standard that simply does not exist. Furthermore, grades rate students against this hypothetical, external standard often with little concern for the actual abilities and accomplishments of the student as a person. Learning is an intimately personal endeavor; grades are highly impersonal. If grades reflect any personality at all, it is that of the teacher/grader, not of the student.

In addition, grades subtly but unquestionably shift the emphasis of learning away from its true aim, and in the process, pit the students against each other as well. The students compete for grades, often with little or no concern for the knowledge that is supposed to be involved. Case in point, we once invited a student to visit WATERSHED to fill our students in on the regular seventh grade social studies curriculum. After listing for ten minutes the topics being covered in her social studies class, the student was asked to expand on one of those topics, Mesopotamia. "Oh," she replied, "I don't remember; we covered that last week: but I know I got an 'A' on the test."

Similarly, some teachers attempt to create an even more concrete illusion of objectivity by implementing complex numerical point systems. Students then supposedly "earn" their grade by accumulating predetermined numbers of these points. Two problems with this procedure come immediately to mind. First, while one can assign points to a test of factual recall, facts per se should not be the end of education. The quality application of information should be that aim, and how does one assign points to a qualitative product? Secondly, and not surprisingly, many of these points can often be earned through behaviors designed to make the teacher's job easier, but which have little or nothing to do with learning itself. Being in class on time; never speaking out of turn; always having a pencil; printing your name in just the "proper" place on each page; skipping lines in essays; (I could go on ad infinitum) any and all of these may earn students points toward a letter grade which is somehow supposed to indicate a command of subject matter.

We have deluded students and parents into believing that grades have some real meaning and intrinsic value.

Then there is always EXTRA CREDIT. In one class, the point difference between letter grades and possibly between passing and failing hinged potentially on whether or not the student wore a "native American" type costume on Halloween. And this supposedly has significance?

Yet, we as an educational system have successfully deluded generations of students, now parents, into believing these grades have some real meaning and intrinsic, objective value. We have done such a complete sales job, for example, that one of our first WATERSHED students once begged us to give her a grade. When asked why, she responded, "I'm doing the best work of my life, and I'd like an 'A' to prove it." To this day, when our students receive a grade/comment report form from their foreign language teacher (class taken outside of WATERSHED), the immediate focus of attention is on the letter grade. Many do not bother to read the comments at all. Both instances represent sad testimony to the "value" of learning which our educational system has instilled in children after just six years of schooling.

...we wanted learning to take place outside the classroom in the real world

We contend that this emphasis on the grade, not the knowledge, leads students to cheat, to plagiarize, and to shortcut assignments. After all, if only the grade is important, the means to achieve that end may not matter very much.

So, grades were out. With no grades in WATERSHED, the students would have to focus on their learning, and they would have to read our comments for feedback.

Next, we knew we wanted learning to take place outside the classroom in the real world. Again, our experiences in the gifted program had shown us just how well students learn when taken out of school and given the chance to see knowledge as it applies to real life situations.

Take, for example, the Academic Excursions Program described briefly in the introduction. Small groups of gifted children who expressed an interest in a particular topic were asked to complete selected readings and answer questions concerning that topic. Once they demonstrated mastery of the readings, usually through one-on-one discussions with me or with Ed, the students were then taken out of school for a day to visit a museum, theater, business, or other location germane to their topic of interest.

These trips proved overwhelmingly successful. Students willingly tackled the extra and often difficult readings for the chance to visit a real life setting pertaining to their chosen topic. Indeed, it was just such an academic excursion that made us realize—if you'll forgive the pun—how natural the watershed topic would be for students. So, the curriculum had to emphasize first-hand, exploratory, on-site learning experiences.

Similarly, we wanted a curriculum that had meaning to the students and topics with which they could associate themselves. Again, the self-determined interest of the students in the Academic Excursion Program, along with the self-determined project structure of our gifted program in general, had adequately demonstrated the obvious but often ignored advantages of tapping into student interests. In short, we knew the program would have to have a central theme that crossed all academic boundaries and also was of interest to the students.

Though we discussed other potential topics, the notion of the watershed quickly rose to the fore. In fact, I can no longer remember what others we considered; that's how much those other topics paled compared to watersheds as far as we were concerned. After the fact, we can now see numerous other topics what would work equally as well and make wonderful central themes. For example, several years into WATERSHED, a student teacher working with us developed plans for a similar whole learning program centered around sports in America. We have also thought through possible programs using central themes such as theater, wellness, and various specific locations—the New Jersey pinelands, or Ithaca, New York, for example. In fact, as we have presented the WATERSHED programs to groups around the country, we have discussed countless possibilities tailored to the locations and needs of our audiences. Almost any topic could be a central theme if properly developed.

At that time, however, watersheds seemed to us the ideal theme around which to build our dream program. We have used it ever since, and we have not regretted our choice.

Since everything physical or societal that occurs within a watershed effects that watershed, a good sized watershed clearly represents a microcosm of the world. As such, any watershed can be examined from every conceivable viewpoint. Furthermore, since everyone lives in a watershed, and as all our actions effect that watershed, we could incorporate any and all student activities and interests into our study.

Once the topic was determined, we explored the logistics of fitting our ideal curriculum into the middle school program. We knew from experience with our Academic Excursions Program that one of our greatest problems would come from other staff members whose classes we would interrupt when we wanted to take students out of the building on trips. Students would miss work, assignments, tests. That could impact on their grades.

And what about crossing class periods? Lessons and activities cannot always be confined to the forty minute periods which comprise Radnor Middle School's daily class schedule. Why should students actively engaged in a particular experience be forced by arbitrary time constraints to switch to a different and usually unrelated experience?

The solution was remarkably simple. Unfortunately, it was also remarkably unspeakable—completely remove the students from the traditional schedule: completely remove the students from other teachers' classes.

But wait, if a student can be removed from social studies class, or science class, or—worst of all—English class, what does that imply about the value of those classes, per se? Once again the answer was as obvious as it was unspeakable. Nonetheless, it seemed absolutely apparent that our ideal program could not, by definition, succeed within the restrictions of the traditional school day. Like traditional grading schemes, the typical schedule of class periods had to go.

...the typical schedule of class periods had to go.

Not surprisingly, this is the issue that continues to cause the most controversy and results in the most resistance we face when we try to convince other teachers to adopt whole learning programs of this sort. Put bluntly, teachers feel threatened when the sanctity of their subject area is questioned. After all, this strikes at the very heart of everything they were taught. I've known teachers who are absolutely convinced that if a students misses his or her class for even a day that student will be irreparably damaged for life. One can only pity the billions of students who, by the bad luck of time or geography, will never have the opportunity to experience that teacher's class.

Furthermore, while jealously guarding the importance of their own limited subject area, many teachers vehemently resist the uncertainties involved in teaching outside their subject area. John Lounsbury of the National Middle School Association refers to this quite appropriately as the teachers' "certification comfort zone."

...all good teachers already possess the skills needed to work outside the scope of their subject.

While these fears may seem insurmountable, they are not. True, one has to redefine one's role as teacher: the teacher is not a dispenser of specific knowledge, but rather a co-learner in an on-going process of searching for answers. This process of looking for solutions transcends all specific disciplines. Consequently, all good teachers already possess the skills needed to work successfully outside the limited scope of their subject area expertise. The only teachers who need realistically fear this type of approach are those who probably should not be in a classroom anyway; namely those who would use their certification to insulate themselves from all changes. I contend that most teachers, if given the opportunity to try teaching beyond their certification comfort zone, are quite capable of doing an excellent job—better, in fact, than they can currently do in the present restrictive educational environment. In addition, most would find it a far more interesting way to work.

So, we took the schedule gridlock back to zero and started over to build a new daily format without subject areas or forty minute class periods.

The next question, how long should the program last? At first, as we had six week reporting periods at R.M.S., we thought about a six week elective. Several problems immediately arose. To begin with, students in the two six week winter periods would not have anywhere near the same experience as those in the fall and spring sessions due to the limitations imposed by the weather and water temperatures. Second, the grade level population would not support six sessions. Though Ed and I would have loved the average group size of twenty-five or so students six sessions would have allowed, we knew that the financial realities of the public school system would never allow it, even in a relatively wealthy district like Radnor. Two teachers sharing twenty-five students would destroy the sacred student-teacher ratio. More important, if every student had to take the program, as six sessions would necessitate, choice and student interest would immediately be lost.

What about a twelve week program, or half the year? This could account for half the grade level population—or even more if the group size went up. But what again of choice and interest? Just as important, where would the students come from and go to for the other two thirds or half the year? Clearly, other teachers and programs would be severely impacted if we were to implement a program in this way.

Again the answer was clear. The program would have to last the entire year. Students would have to be willing to pull out of the traditional program for a whole year.

What then about class size? This is a volatile issue. Too few students would provoke accusations of disparity from other teachers and their union who continue to define teaching in the traditional way. Too many students would cause logistical and safety concerns.

Our principal advised that we opt for forty students. This number, seen—albeit incorrectly—as twenty students per teacher, would be close enough to the district average of 22:1, yet would also be a workable number in terms of classroom space and field study logistics. We would have preferred a maximum of thirty students; a number which would be quite feasible for all teams if our entire school were reorganized along WATERSHED lines. Nevertheless, to get the program going, we compromised at forty.

Yet, this brings to the front the entire issue of teacher:student ratios. Critics of our whole learning approach and advocates of traditional assembly line educational practices argue for more students per teacher. How many times have we heard the claim: "Back in my day we had fifty kids in the class, and the teacher did just fine"? Current fiscal concerns make this argument seem all the more attractive, particularly to those who have never tried to teach, to those whose selective memories have allowed them to forget just what a miserable experience that large class was for them as students, or to those who have not given much serious thought to the aims of education. If memorization of unrelated, insignificant facts is all you want a child to be able to do, the old system might appear to work. Actually, I have my doubts. Put simply, the world has changed too much since "back in my day," and time does not go in reverse.

Yet, even more important, no reasonable person would continue to argue that memorization is the goal of education. The goal is thinking; that is, using information to solve ever-changing problems under ever-changing conditions. The process of education must reflect this goal: the means must embody this end. In short, the very medium of education must simultaneously be its message.

This medium, this type of process by definition cannot be assembly line in nature. It requires techniques which stimulate exploration, discussion, and experimentation. It demands dynamic interaction among teachers and students.

The program would have to last the entire year.

...the very medium of education must simultaneously be its message.

If this dynamism is given its proper place, it becomes the limiting factor for group size. How many students can a teacher get to know well enough and long enough to let this process develop and thrive?

Here is where other factors come to bear. For example, if the present schedule practices are maintained so a given teacher has only a limited forty minutes or so per day with a group of students, the number of students per group ought, by rights, drop from the current twenty-plus levels to about twelve. Obviously, this would necessitate a tremendous increase in the teaching staff of most schools and would be financially impractical to implement. Besides, and perhaps needless to add, this idea would still fail to address the basic problem inherent in education through isolated disciplines.

If, however, a total restructuring such as the one used in WATER-SHED were adopted, the process could be achieved without greatly increasing staff levels. Again, this is predicated on two basic points: first, small teams of teachers must have a small group of students for a significantly longer period of time each day; and second, the curriculum should be holistically based focused on a central theme, not subject area content. Again, if totally reorganized along WATERSHED lines, our school could operate more effectively with little or no increase in staff levels.

By the end of that November 1985 in-service day we had formalized our thinking on most of these points. Not wanting to have to reinvent the wheel, we began to search for existing programs from which we could learn. Reminiscent of our search for a canoe trailer, we quickly learned that we would have to create our own. Programs from places as diverse as Washington state and Connecticut answered our inquiries, but they were usually limited in scope to the environmental sciences and in time to a class period per day at best. Many "programs" were merely two week mini-units. Nothing we could find evinced the range of experiences and time commitment we sought. We were on our own.

Once we cleared the hurdle this realization represented, we found ourselves remarkably free to be creative in our approach to the development of content and activities.

In our search, Ed and I met many people who wanted to help. Everywhere we went people were excited by the potential they saw in our ideas. Many encouraged us and offered helpful information and further contacts. As a rule, we found most people were anxious to help. Almost everyone has some type of expertise and would love to share if only someone would ask. I'm sure other teachers trying to initiate similar programs will find the same is true everywhere. Special credit, however, goes to Bob Struble, the executive director of the Brandywine Valley Association, America's first watershed association. Not only did Bob encourage us and introduce us to others who could help, he also gave us an opportunity to pilot some of our ideas in a two week long summer session at the BVA's summer day camp. That experience, which we called "The Brandywine Saga," enabled us to polish ideas and techniques we thought would work, and to throw out a few we discovered would not work. Tangentially, that summer program continues to this day; and for the past few years has involved a teacher training component along with the students.

At any rate, by December of 1985, we had formalized a tentative scope and sequence; and we had developed activities in sufficient detail to share with our principal, Anne Janson. She, in turn, requested that we share our idea at that point with the Board of School Directors, and we found ourselves on the agenda for the February 1986 general board meeting.

A brief word about the Radnor Board of School Directors circa 1985-86: they were not known for their generosity or for their receptiveness to new ideas. In fact, some of the board members were infamous for their thriftiness and their conservatism. "Back to Basics?" Some of these citizens thought that they invented the concept! In response to the numerous critiques of American education which appeared in the first half of the 1980s, the Board generally called for more tests, more discipline, more homework; in short, more of the same old same old.

Little wonder that I remember perspiring profusely despite the February chill as Ed and I met in the parking lot that evening and then ventured into the board room. As we were not first on the evening's docket, we sweated through several other business matters, none of which I can now recall.

Finally our turn came. School Board protocol required that the acting assistant to the superintendent introduce us. This gentleman, who has since become one of our sincerest advocates, was at that time striving to keep his political options afloat on a turbulent sea of administrative job changes. He stepped confidently to the center of the room and announced to the Board members, "I know you're probably not going to approve this proposed program, but these men have worked hard on it; so I think you should hear their idea."

With such sterling approbation, how could we lose?

For the next forty-five minutes or so we presented our basic plan, a copy of which appears as Appendix A in this book. In brief, we proposed to work with forty randomly selected seventh graders representing all ability levels. This group would devote its entire school year, all day, every day, to the comprehensive study of a specific watershed. The skills and concepts covered in the traditional disciplines would be focused on to this river study. Elements of English, math, social studies, science, humanities, reading, art, music, and physical education would be included and reintegrated. Classroom activities would center around various research projects designed to examine the watershed from all points of view. These projects would be enhanced by guest speakers and field trips.

In addition, as much time as possible would be spent on the stream. The students would put to first-hand, practical use the skills and concepts they acquired in the classroom when they walked and canoed the stream's entire length in a series of field trips. Students would, for example, measure and map selected portions of the stream; perform chemical tests and physical measurements; calculate a biotic index of benthic invertebrates; observe and describe the plants and animals encountered; and then record all their results, observations, experiences, and reactions in writing, on film, and through art.

...as much time as possible would be spent on the stream.

Once we finished outlining our overview, we fielded questions. For the most part, these questions were positive and constructive.

Of major concern, as we had anticipated, was the issue of math. Because math is the one subject most truly sequenced in a significant way,

Chemical tests were performed on water samples and data recorded.

the Board wanted to ensure that no student in our program would lose ground. The Board, as we expected, was convinced that this could only be guaranteed if math instruction remained in the hands of a certified math teacher. So, we consented to the idea that math could remain a separate subject around which we would work if the pilot program gained approval.

Tangentially, and at the risk of getting ahead of the story a bit, we have since that time made great strides, with the help of our math teacher, toward the integration of math into the WATERSHED program. I continue to believe that math can indeed be taught successfully as part of the integrated whole. Each year we have moved a little closer to that goal as our math teacher has collaborated with us on new activities and strategies involving math.

Our principal testified that approval from the State Board of Education would not be a problem. Our proposed program contained within it all the elements required by the State; and, because middle schools remain an experimental form in Pennsylvania, our respective teacher certifications and experiences permitted us to teach a variety of subjects at the middle school level. (After all, any good teacher ought to be capable of teaching any topic, particularly at a middle school level. Once we abandon the notion of subject area curricula, the act of teaching ceases to be based on the teacher who "knows" the answer. It changes instead to a process orientation which requires teachers to know how to find answers and information, the very skills we want our students to learn, the same skills they will need to survive in the twenty-first century. Subject area certification becomes less meaningful and should not stand in the way of innovative programs.)

What about liability? Surely a program such as the one we proposed entailed significant risks? Again Anne Janson came to the rescue. She had already confirmed with the district's solicitors that the District had more than adequate coverage. That, combined with the parents' involvement in the program and with the emphasis to be placed on safety in the program, reduced the risks of legal difficulties. The legal hurdles thus cleared, the Board asked their last question: "Can you start this coming September?" A flattering proposition, to be sure, and a tempting one as well; but we opted for an additional year to flesh out our planning and work out all the logistics.

And so it began. For the next eighteen months Ed and I devoted every possible "free" moment to developing specific plans and activities.

During this time, we were assigned a physical location for our program. As we would be working with forty students, we needed a larger that normal space. Two back corner rooms on the second floor of our three story building had a folding wall between them. With this wall folded completely back, the two rooms became one large "L" shaped space. Perfect. That this space was on a back corner, our nearest neighbor being the auditorium balcony, meant that we would not disturb many others. As an added bonus, the room abutted a stairwell leading to an outside entrance: we could come and go on our many trips with an equally minimal amount of disruption.

We would like to have had running water available in the room, but a lavatory and a janitor's closet were directly across the hall anyway. A phone with an outside line would have been nice as well; but then we were probably just spoiled by having had one in our room for the gifted program. We could get by without a phone. In short, the space was perfect, and having a space made the program seem that much more real.

Tangentially, in subsequent years we had a phone line installed. It proved essential for making arrangements for trips and guest speakers. I would recommend that any whole learning program should have a phone, and nowadays a fax and a modem as well. Similarly, we also added the luxury of sinks and water when we moved to a new location in year four; but I'm getting too far ahead of the story.

The other "space" we needed was a watershed. Actually, this choice had been made even before our presentation to the Board. Though our ultimate goal was to study different watersheds in different years—a goal we have since fulfilled—the logical choice, we felt, for starting the program had to be the Brandywine. We already had a fair amount of experience with this river through our Academic Excursions and later through the continuing Brandywine Saga summer program. The river offered many easily accessible sites. It had cultural and historical significance. It was canoeable. It offered us a wide variety of support resources such as the Brandywine Valley Association and the Brandywine Conservancy. It represented the perfect choice. So, the Brandywine it would be.

"The Brandywine at Hibernia" by Jamie Lewis, 1990

We needed just one more element to make the program an actuality; the most important ingredient of all, students.

Our experiences with the gifted program sensitized us to the issues and dangers of various selection processes. We did not want the program viewed as elitist in any way. We wanted everyone who so wanted to be equally eligible to participate. Furthermore, to avoid any possible claim or even suspicion of favoritism, we did not want to be personally involved in the selection process at all. Yet, we also knew that we were going to be asking a great deal of a group of students and their parents. We were asking them to accept a major academic risk on little more than our personal reputations as teachers. We were not sure anyone would choose to go up the creek with us.

Weighing all the factors, we decided to let a computer randomize the entire sixth grade class and generate a list of candidates. From this list, the first twenty boys and the first twenty girls were identified as priority participants. Ten additional boys and ten additional girls were selected, in order, from the computer's list to be alternates should priority candidates elect not to participate.

The decision to balance the class with boys and girls was a conscious one, and one which we continue to this day. We have been confronted with good arguments against this; namely that the group is, in a backhanded way, gender biased by a sort of quota system. While this may appear to be true, our motives for the balance are quite different. Our mutual experience with middle school children has amply demonstrated that the students feel uncomfortable in groups where girls outnumber boys or boys outnumber girls. When given a choice to form groups of their own, seventh grade students seem generally to group themselves with others of their own sex. When asked or required to have coed groups, they will generally demand equal numbers of boys and girls. So, it was and is with this student preference in mind that we maintain a balance of boys and girls in the class.

At any rate, all sixty of the computer identified students, along with their parents, received an invitation by letter to attend a special meeting to hear about our plans, ask questions, and be given the opportunity to decide whether or not they wished to participate. The invitation further stipulated that failure to attend the meeting would be interpreted as an "a priori" decision not to participate, and that child's name would be removed from the list.

We held the meeting in the Commons, a large open room just inside the entrance to the building from the bus driveway. (Ironically, this space, with some significant alterations, became the WATERSHED classroom during the fourth year of the program and remains so to this day.) As the parents and students arrived, each family received a card on which they were to state their final decision about participating. They were to return this response card card within a week after the meeting.

Staring out across a sea of about 200 people that evening, I felt much as Peter Minuit must have felt one evening 350 years before in 1637. Like Minuit, who was about to launch Sweden's first colonial expedition to the New World, we stood face-to-face with an unknown future. Like Minuit, Ed and I had to convince these people that the voyage into that future would be sufficiently safe and profitable to merit the obvious risks involved. Minuit convinced a handful of Swedes and Finns to go with him. We somehow succeeded in convincing all but a few of the designated participants, and all of the alternates, to join us.

We introduced ourselves, showed slides from our summer Brandywine Saga program, outlined our plans for the year, and answered questions. Many of the questions were the same ones we continue to confront today. What are the students "missing" from the regular curriculum? Will my child be safe? What about math? When will the students do English? If you don't give grades, how will we know how our child is doing? Will my child fall behind the students in the regular program? What about test-taking skills? Will this cost us more? And so on, and so forth.

The meeting lasted about two hours. When it was over, numerous parents came up to ask individual questions and to express their gratitude for having been granted the opportunity to participate. Though they had been given a week to make up their mind, most turned in their response card that evening. The alternates all wanted to be in, and they anxiously awaited news of any designated participant who might decline his or her invitation. Few did.

Each future Watersheder received a summer packet.

Within a week the list was complete. Each future Watersheder received a summer packet which included selected readings , maps, vocabulary lists, an interest survey and a commitment pledge. These materials were to be read and completed before the opening of school in September. The packet also included a stamped postcard which we asked the students to send back to us at some point during the summer to let us know what they were doing.

This summer packet served many purposes, and it continues to be an important part of the whole WATERSHED process. First, it gives the students a chance to familiarize themselves with terms and concepts we will be using throughout the year, right from the very first day. At the same time, it keeps them thinking, reading, and writing over the summer; and it gives them a common task. That, together with the postcard, gives the students an important sense of belonging even before the school year begins. This makes their transition into WATERSHED a smoother one for us all. You will find examples from the Summer Packets in Appendix B.

And so, like Peter Minuit, we had our crew—in fact, a group just slightly larger than his—and we set sail, so to speak, on a remarkable adventure which continues to this day. Over the intervening years we have witnessed our share of storms and doldrums, and we have enjoyed wonderful times of smooth sailing. We have experienced success, and we have felt failure. We have watched little ideas blossom, and we have seen grand ideas wither. We have made adjustments, as you will see in the coming chapters, but I believe we remain as true as ever to the course we set back then in 1987.

Along the way, I have learned a great deal. I have learned more about this region of southeastern Pennsylvania that I ever thought possible—and I'm a twelfth generation native of the area descended from those early Swedish settlers. I have learned more that I ever wanted to learn about the inefficiencies and injustices of the American system of education as it currently exists. I have discovered many of my own weaknesses, and I hope a few strengths. I have learned a few things about seventh graders; primarily that I still don't know much about them, and that they continue to amaze and frustrate me each and every day.

Most of all, I've learned that learning is truly a journey, without beginning or end, that weaves us all together among the senses of place, time and quality which constitute our identity. We cannot separate the journey from the destination, or the traveler from the path. **W**

Wild Indians and a Sense of Place

2.

Lenape of the Unami Sib
(Turtle)

ERICA
DOMESEK
'94

I have learned that seventh graders clearly have much in common with wild Indians—primarily, I suspect, the poor image they seem to have with almost everyone else. Yet, beyond the undeserved stereotypes, our seventh graders share many more meaningful characteristics with the Lenni-Lenape who inhabited the Delaware River valley for at least three and a half thousand years prior to Columbus.

For one thing, the "Original People," as they called themselves, loved the land. The valley was theirs although—or maybe because—they did not own it. Our students, at first enthralled merely with the idea of the WATERSHED program, soon came to love it and the land we studied as well—though they obviously do not own any of it. On a family canoe trip at the end of our first year, a parent experiencing the Brandywine River for the first time remarked how beautiful it was. Responding to her mother, a student simply said, "Thank you." Clearly that student sensed an ownership of the river that no written deed or writ of riparian rights could ever express. In much the same way, the Lenape held the land without a need for legal ownership.

In fact, the native Americans were at first mystified by the white men's tract boundaries and deeds. The sachems, clan spokesmen, must have received with amused wonder the Europeans' metal pots and knives, axes and glass beads presented in exchange for a commodity as free to all as the air. Beaver pelts and wampum shells could be accumulated or traded; a clay pipe could be owned and treasured, shown off and flaunted; but land— well, land was simply there. People, animals and spirit ancestors all shared the same space.

The space the Lenape shared among their twelve sibs, or clans, stretched from modern day New York to Maryland. The Lenape were part of the larger "Delaware" tribe of the still larger Algonquin family, a family based primarily on a common language . By and large, the Lenape were peaceful farmers and fishers, not savage warriors as Native Americans are so often depicted on TV and movie screens. Their complex, matrilineal society was highly refined and cultured, though not technologically advanced when measured by the European standards of the day.

Most Lenape settlements were small and seasonal, a fact which later caused them great difficulty in their dealings with the English. Several larger towns existed in this area, however, long before the arrival of the Swedes and the Dutch in the early 1600's. Perhaps the largest of these was Shackamaxon located along the Delaware River within the limits of present day Philadelphia. This town thrived as a center for Lenape commerce and culture, and many of today's major highways such as Routes 1, 3, 30, and I-95 follow the original Lenape trails such as the Great Minquas Path and the Allegheny Path which connected Shackamaxon with other Lenape villages.

Another important town, Katamoonchinck, located northeast of modern day West Chester in the fertile South Valley, or "Great Valley" as people around here call it now, probably served as a farming center. Queonemysing, in the "Big Bend," where the Brandywine River dips in, then out, then back into the state of Delaware, was primarily a fishing village. Plentiful shad provided a major food source for the three to five hundred Lenape of the Unami, or Turtle, sib who lived peacefully along the Brandywine's banks.

BRANDYWINE MAN

By Chuck MARDEN '87

These villages and all the land surrounding them belonged to everyone in the sib. Thus, while the Lenape felt a general sense of clan territory, no fences separated wigwams; no hedgerows divided parcels of sown fields.

Similarly, since no Lenape claimed ownership of a particular acreage, no individual Lenape felt compelled to "improve" any specific piece of the landscape. The Lenape used the land in a particular spot until it no longer provided for them. Then they moved on to another site nearby and allowed their former site to revitalize itself naturally.

Over the centuries, the Lenape established a pattern of seasonal migrations from site to site. They spent springs and summers in their fishing and farming villages near the rivers and creeks, or near the shore where they could collect shellfish. Then, after their autumnal harvest ceremonies, they moved to wintering sites on higher and more sheltered grounds, usually just a few miles away. With spring's fish spawning runs, the Lenape returned to their river campsites.

Early European settlers had difficulty comprehending these patterns and attitudes. To the European mind, private ownership of land was not only possible, it was desirable. Land meant wealth, prestige and power. Indeed, the promise of land ownership, even in a wilderness, served as a primary attraction drawing settlers away from the stagnant system of landed gentry in Europe. This was particularly true in Pennsylvania where, by the early 1700's, the liberal Quakers encouraged land ownership for everyone.

Additionally, land ownership carried with it implicit responsibilities. Most notably, Europeans believed that the prerogatives of land ownership required one to improve one's land. Unimproved acreage rapidly became fair game for squatters: that is, for any person willing to invest time and effort (if not money) to make the land better. Of course, the very term "better" as used here implies a human domination of the land; a notion totally alien to the Lenape, and a tacit belief rooted perhaps in the same hierarchical world view which led Europeans to consider non-Christians as something less than human.

Thus, the poor Lenape did not stand a chance. First, they were not God's chosen: even those who elected to abandon their native animism did not quite qualify for equal treatment by God or man. Second, these "poor Rogues," as Johan Printz, governor of New Sweden, called them, left sites seasonally, thus failing (in the Europeans' eyes) to improve the land. Obviously the Lenape forfeited their rights to the land. The settlers could confiscate it with clear conscience, which they frequently did regardless of treaty arrangements designed at first by Minuit and later by William Penn and his agents to preserve Lenape rights. That this might be unjust was by all European counts inconceivable.

Just as their Lenape predecessors held beliefs that the Europeans found incomprehensible, seventh graders hold ideas concerning space and territoriality that defy adult understanding. On the one hand, all property is communal. One's belongings can legitimately be stored anywhere within the general territory of our room—that is, until another person decides he or she needs that property, at which point communal ownership immediately gives way to the private sector. This proved a major area of concern for us all as we groped our way through that first year together. It continues to present interesting situations.

Students frequently borrow each other's materials without asking, and, with equal frequency, become outraged when someone else does the same to them. This problem is compounded by the daily (sometimes hourly) shifting of personal alliances. One day a "best" friend may borrow something without asking; the next day not. We have convened numerous group meetings—we call them "rug meetings" because we all sit in a circle on the floor to discuss serious matters of this sort—over the years to discuss this particular issue and ways to handle it. The students always vow to change their behavior, and they usually manage to keep their promise, at least for a day or two. That's when we keep reminding ourselves that the victory, the learning, is in the struggle.

Classroom materials are a similar case. That first year, stockpiled materials that Ed and I expected to last the year disappeared by the end of September. Forty pairs of scissors vanished, reappeared, and vanished again; and no one had any idea at times where even a single pair might be. Four dozen rulers, six bottles of rubber cement, several sets of markers and colored pencils…the list goes on. We started referring to certain areas of the room as the Brandywine Triangle. Had the Lenape still lived nearby, I would have suspected that some serious land speculation had occurred, and that some sachem sat by his fire proudly showing off the wonders of scotch tape and staplers.

Coincidentally, almost all the scissors, rulers, and staplers magically reappeared the last day of school. I remember one student in particular: during the school year he was always complaining that he needed a ruler but couldn't find one. We found eight rulers in his desk on the closing day of school. This general pattern repeats itself annually, just like the Lenape cycle of seasonal migration.

We also learned that the twelve year old mind holds some pretty clear cut notions about personal space. Ed and I had a grand scheme concerning communal space when we began our planning for WATERSHED. We believe the room belongs to everyone in the program, a concept we continue to espouse. As a part of this belief, we did away with teachers' desks. Furniture, after all, makes definite statements, and the traditional "teacher's desk " constitutes a heavy authority symbol. It also provides an all too convenient place of retreat. So, we threw out our desks.

We wanted an active space.

In preparation for that first WATERSHED year, we did the same with the students' desks as well. In their place we scattered several large tables about the room and twenty chairs—obviously not enough for all our forty students to sit at once. We wanted an active space, a place where students moved about and interacted with each other continually. Being sensitive, or so we thought, to the student's need for some place to put personal items, we provided each student with a cardboard storage box. My son and I spent an entire summer day inserting tab "A:" into slot "B" for forty such boxes.

These boxes lasted, in various conditions, until December. By then it was clear that our ideas about place and space required a slight readjustment to bring them in line with the students' ideas. First of all, the boxes simply were not sturdy enough to withstand the necessary abuse they suffered each day. Many caved in before the end of the first month. Lids continually disappeared. Contents spilled. After the novelty and the initial thrill of personalizing the boxes wore off, the students hated them. Furthermore, the boxes and lids were always underfoot. More than once I tripped over a box left unattended in the middle of the floor.

So, we abandoned the boxes, as the Lenape abandoned over-used fields. We replaced them one December afternoon with forty old elementary school desks, the kind with a large, deep storage compartment under the lift-up writing surface. We had found the desks piled up in a sub-basement storage room like the remnants of a Lenape clambake. It required two hours of strenuous work to extricate the desks and carry them up the four long flights of stairs to the WATERSHED room.

That problem solved, we confronted our next dilemma: how should these desks be arranged in the room? Having just grudgingly conceded the very need for this furniture, Ed and I were not willing to see the desks lined up in staid rows reminiscent of the traditional classroom. Several visiting high school students came to our rescue. As I recall, they grouped the desks so as to spell out their boyfriends' names.

At any rate, our students were overjoyed when they arrived the following morning. It was like Christmas. In fact, it was just about Christmas. They staked claims at once, transferred belongings from dilapidated boxes, and erased the carefully arranged names in favor of their own groupings.

Since then the desks have been an integral part of the program. The students move them at will, as needs and alliances change, often in cycles, again reminiscent of the Lenape. Interestingly, in seven years the students have never once chosen to put the desks in traditional rows.

...a place where students could work with one another.

To this day, only Ed and I have staunchly refused to readopt desks. We have, however, resorted to using a large table from time to time as a space for working with students, as a place to stack papers, and as a general gathering place for just about everyone who enters the room. Still, old habits die hard. Despite our best efforts, we find ourselves too frequently and too comfortably anchored to the table. So, we move the table periodically. I think the Lenape would approve. ⨳

Even reference books are used in the outdoor classroom.

Explorations: The First Year

3.

The "Kalmar Nyckel" drawing by Erika Bausman '94

Had public school existed at that time, twelve year old Princess Christina would have been in seventh grade in 1638 when she, along with her advisors, decided to start a colony in North America.

Her father, King Gustavus Adolphus, had died in 1632. At that time the six year old princess was far too young to rule a leading European military power. So, she was aided in that task by her prime minister, Axel Oxenstierna, until she reached her majority. During that period plans were formalized, the New Sweden Company established, an expedition launched.

Peter Minuit, of New Netherlands fame, signed on to lead that expedition. After purchasing Manhattan for the bargain price of twenty-four dollars worth of beads and trinkets, Minuit had become disgruntled with his Dutch employers, or they with him. Either way, Minuit was relieved of his command and recalled to Holland. It probably did not require much coaxing to convince him to sell his leadership expertise and his knowledge of North America to the Swedish crown; particularly when he knew he would be establishing his newest venture right under the noses of his former employers.

In two small ships, the *Kalmar Nyckel* and the *Fogel Grip,* Minuit and his crew set sail from Gothenburg in November of 1637. Storms in the North Sea damaged both vessels and forced the expedition to put into a Dutch port for repairs. On New Year's Eve, 1637, Minuit's ships again set sail. By early March he had successfully negotiated the Atlantic and reached the mouth of the South River, today known as the Delaware River.

Knowing that the Dutch had small trading posts along the eastern banks of the river, in the area of present day Trenton, New Jersey, Minuit chose to locate his settlement on the western side of the river.

Sailing up the Delaware River from the ocean about forty miles, Minuit found again the mouth of a smaller, sluggish, tidewater stream. At that time the stream was called Minquaskill after the tribe of Susquehannock Indians who lived along its westernmost headwaters. Minuit probably knew this deep water stream from earlier explorations out of New Amsterdam. He likely knew as well of the natural rock ledge a quarter of a mile up the Minquaskill, just out of sight of any Dutch ships that might pass along the Delaware, and just past the confluence of another small stream, the Fiskekill. This area of flat rocks would make a perfect wharf off which to moor his ships. The Fiskekill, today called the Brandywine, being a fall line stream, offered bountiful resources of fresh water, energy, and fish.

By the 29th of March, Minuit had met with local Lenape and Nanticoke sachems and had negotiated a deal for land. Sweden now controlled all the land west of the Delaware River from Duck Creek, near Bombay Hook, north to the Schuylkill River. Minuit built a small fort, which he appropriately named Fort Christina. He armed it with several cannons from the *Kalmar Nyckel,* garrisoned it with twenty-four settlers, and then set sail for the West Indies to do a little trading or pirating.

All was going according to plan.

All went according to plan for Ed and me that summer of 1987. Once again we conducted our Brandywine Saga program at BVA. We refined old ideas and developed new ones. We set up our new room, as sparsely furnished as Fort Christina probably was in its first year. We planned trips. We laid out the first six weeks of classroom time in minute detail. We were ready.

Minuit could not have been more excited or more sure of himself as he set foot for the first time in New Sweden than we were as the 1987 school year opened.

All seventh grade students and staff gathered in the main gym as usual that first morning. Teachers greeted familiar faces and helped direct and reassure new ones. After the assistant principal's traditional-first-day-of-school-obligatory-welcoming remarks, it was time for each homeroom teacher to step forward and read out his or her class list. The teacher then escorted that group back to their new homeroom where a plethora of traditional-first-day-of-school-fill-out-these forms awaited them. At this point, Ed and I stepped in. Instead of reading out forty names, however, we simply called for the Brandywine WATERSHED group to follow us outside. These students already had a group identity. They were as different from the other seventh graders at that point as the Swedish settlers were from the Lenape. This identity proved both a blessing and a bane as that year and subsequent years progressed—but more on that later.

Once outside, we took the first of many group photographs, and then we formed a large circle for some cooperative games designed to help us get to know one another. While the rest of the school labored over ludicrous forms, we "passed the pulse," made human springs, and began learning to depend on each other. Then, in small groups, we transported water using different utensils such as sponges, spoons, and straws. We measured the amount of water carried, and we recorded the advantages and disadvantages of each utensil. Sitting in a circle on the softball field while others sat in hot classrooms, we discussed our results and learned about the pitfalls in taking and recording accurate measurements. We also began learning about the advantages of cooperation.

Once inside the room, the students became true explorers. Like those first Swedish colonists, the students mapped areas of their new home and discovered where resources were located. Next they were given five minutes to find facts about water, and then we shared these facts. Even I learned a thing or two! Most important, however, the students took possession of their room through this shared experience, and the cooperative tone was established.

...the students took possession of their room...and the cooperative tone was established.

This tone was reinforced as we held our first "Rug Meeting" to discuss the coming tear's experiment in whole learning. None of us knew quite what to expect. What would it be like to spend the next year together, all day, every day in a fairly confined space? In a very real sense we were like those early settlers. And like those colonists, we would have to depend heavily on each other for support and tolerance in the face of

external difficulties and internal problems. The students developed a sophisticated list of guidelines for getting along. The list began with the simple phrase, "Be Nice." We made a poster of these guidelines and hung it on the wall near our "Five C's" of Cooperation, Caring, Caution, Commitment and Caring" (Jacobson, 1987)—the basic tenets of the WATERSHED program which we had adopted from an article by Cliff Jacobson.

Then we played some trust games, such as "Cookie Factory" and "Trust Fall," to bring home the point. In both these games students physically support and protect each other.

In addition, we assigned the first two research projects of the year.

...the students mapped areas of their new home...

The first was a structured phrase outline about a plant we would encounter in the region. The second was a sentence outline about an indigenous animal. The instructions for these reports are included in Appendix C. It is important to note that the reports were sequenced to improve both research and writing skills in addition to introducing content information. In subsequent years, as we moved away from the first year's report format, the writing sequence was presented through other activities such as the Tuesday Tasks we introduced in Year Six.

We ended that first day with time for the students to write a log entry. Though the particular structure has changed several times, to this day we continue to require the students to record daily their accomplishments and the events of each day. After this log time, we came together for a sharing circle to discuss our reactions to that first day. By three o'clock we had done more that I thought we would. I was truly impressed by the students' enthusiasm and their willingness to cooperate, to listen, and to learn.

The obligatory school forms? We assigned them for homework, and almost all came in the next day.

For our part, even though we had accomplished all we had set out to accomplish that first day, Ed and I quickly realized that most of our intricately designed plans would be useless. The forty personalities changed our priorities. The specific plans hit the recycling bin; only the general outline remained as we realized that the program would necessarily have to be flexible to meet local conditions. Minuit had instructions from Queen Christina and her prime minister to accomplish certain general objectives such as growing tobacco, trading for beaver pelts, mapping the area, and raising silkworms. Once in New Sweden, however, Minuit had to adjust his expectations to the conditions he found here. His silkworm project, for example, proved a dismal failure! In much the same way, we could retain our larger set of goals, but we would have to adjust to our new frontier right along with the students.

Once again, the lack of preconceived structures ultimately proved a blessing. It enabled us to experiment freely with new projects and new ideas. Some of these worked incredibly well, some did not.

Minuit had his silkworms; we had our plans for a WATERSHED book. Our original pilot idea, as we presented it to the School Board, centered around the culminating experience of a student-produced book about the Brandywine and our group's experiences on it. Fortunately, our primary mentor on the Board advised us not to count too heavily on this aspect of the program.

We started the year with the notion that the students would decide the form and the content of this book. Early on we introduced this notion to the students and asked them to submit to us general plans or ideas concerning the direction the book should take.

Unfortunately, in September seventh graders could not grasp the vision involved. Very few ideas were submitted, and most of those were unrealistic. Several held possibilities, but the class as a whole could not agree on which they liked best and wanted to pursue.

So, we opted to try parallel productions with volunteers working on the version of their choice. As work progressed we would re-evaluate each version and either eliminate one or merge them closer to the end of the year.

To make a long story short, this plan did not work. By the year's end only one or two students had put any serious effort into the book, and we were forced to settle for a chronological anthology of student writing and art work.

I suppose I should not complain too much. This anthology, while not what we had envisioned, still represented some remarkably fine work by the students. Furthermore, the process involved was as important as the product, though tougher to evaluate. In that sense we succeeded far better than Minuit's early colonists did with their silkworms!

Other projects brought us more readily apparent rewards. One such project was our three-dimensional topographical map of the Brandywine watershed, all 330 square miles of it in U.S.G.S. seven and one half mile scale. We divided the area into forty segments, each about ten inches by ten inches, though none was a perfect square in shape. Each student then took the responsibility to trace and color code by elevation the fifty foot index contours within his or her segment. These tracings were then transferred to corrugated cardboard provided by the local appliance store owner whose daughter was among our first Watersheders.

The students laboriously cut out these cardboard layers of elevation, stacked them together in the proper order, and glued them together to form a step-like model of each map segment. As the elevations within the Brandywine watershed ranged from near sea level at the river's mouth in Wilmington to almost 1100 feet in the Welsh Hills, this meant some segments required as many as twenty-one layers of cardboard.

Through it all the students learned a great deal about maps and about the topography of the Brandywine watershed. One young man who experienced particular difficulty with the tracing and cutting of his layers, finally stacked them together for the first time and promptly announced with genuine amazement, "Hey, these layers show us the shape of the hills!" While we had told him this many times, without the physical act of building those hills, that young man might have studied geography for years—he might even have passed objective tests—and never truly internalized the concept of contour lines or topographical maps.

As you can imagine, the project took months of work; but keep in mind that the students worked on their segments when they wanted to. With just a few exceptions, we did not require map work to be done at specified times. This is part of our strategy to help the students learn to manage their time and accept responsibility for their work.

Then came a truly magical day in January. Though not all the segments were finished, several of us began to play around on the floor with those segments that were completed. Even though we had marked each piece on its underside with compass orientation and general position, the project was still a giant jigsaw puzzle complicated by uneven edges, missing sections and various minor errors. Nevertheless, the map came together for the first time that day, and you could not have found prouder students anywhere—or prouder teachers!

The students laboriously cut out cardboard layers, stacked them, and glued them together to form a step-like model.

This pride resulted in the rapid completion of the remaining pieces and the careful assembly of the entire map. Errors were corrected, edges evened and matched, and the pieces joined together with liberal amounts of white glue. The map, when mounted, covered most of a four foot by eight foot sheet of three quarter inch thick plywood.

The next step was every child's mud pie-dream and every adult's sand castle dream remembered. The entire map surface received several successive layers of plaster spackling compound. As with mud pies and sand castles, no tool but the human hand would do for this job!

The cardboard steps disappeared as the hills and dales of the Piedmont, along with the Great Valley, the fall line, and the coastal plain emerged in winteresque, snow-covered splendor. As March 1988 arrived, the snow white of the plaster vanished, replaced by rich acrylic shades of greens, yellows, ochers, and umbers. The scaled watershed became one of permanent summer.

One morning just a day or so after the map had received its final touches, Ed and I entered the room as usual about 7:15. The bright spring sun, having just cleared the roofs and trees to the east of the school, almost blinded us. As our eyes adjusted to the light, we looked at the map which lay across several desktops. It just happened to be oriented in exactly the correct position, and the sun's light illuminated the map's contours with eerie realism. Even the photograph we took to record the sight does not do justice to the spectacular scene it made. Those early colonists seeing land for the first time after eight weeks at sea could not have been more awed by the landscape spreading out before them.

Today that map is on display at the Brandywine Valley Association's education center where thousands of people, young and old, who visit the Browning Barn can enjoy it, learn from it, and appreciate the remarkable accomplishments of which seventh graders are capable. Every year since then we have made such maps of the watersheds we study. To date, that makes a total of three Brandywine Maps; one each of the smaller Chester, Ridley, Crum, Darby, and Mill creeks; all of which were made cooperatively. For the past three years we have also had each student make his or her own three dimensional map of the tiny Gulph Creek watershed. While each and everyone of these maps impresses me, I must admit that none has had quite the same impact on me as did that original one.

In addition to that particularly successful portion of our original plan, we were also able to implement the series of ten sequenced reports. We began, as mentioned previously, with a phrase outline report on a plant and then a sentence outline report on an animal indigenous to the region. These two highly pre-structured outlines, accompanied by drawings, became the topics for the first of many oral presentations delivered that year by the students.

Report three required the students to write paragraphs describing an assigned geoscience subject of importance to the area. We gave the students the topic question for each paragraph, but they had to develop their own outlines.

For a slight change of pace, report four consisted of a letter for our Adopt-A-Guest portion of the program. Each student had to select a person from a list we had, write to this person, and invite him or her to come in to speak to the class. The letter, in addition to using proper letter form, had to explain to the potential guests what WATERSHED was about and why we wished this person to tell us about his or her occupation.

This proved to be one of the greatest assignments of the year. The students wrote to all kinds of people, and most people responded enthusiastically. Though he could not arrange to come visit, artist Jamie Wyeth, for example, answered one young man's letter which included some questions about a particular painting. A well known Philadelphia area developer, famous for the design and construction of some of Philadelphia's tallest buildings, took the time to come in and talk to the class about planned developments and regional planning. An area horse breeder responded to his Adopt-A-Guest letter by inviting the class to spend a day at his large horse farm where we learned more than you can imagine about one of this area's important industries. We had a biologist from the U.S.G.S. come in and speak about benthic invertebrates and the biotic indexing procedures used professionally to evaluate the health of local streams. A local artist visited and discussed the Brandywine tradition of art. Bob Struble of the Brandywine Valley Association shared his world-class expertise in solid waste management and recycling. These just to name a few of the many guests who visited that first year, and each at the specific invitation of a student who then acted as the guest's host.

"Box Elder"
drawing from a
plant report by
Jamie Kontis '90.

Clearly, this type of project embodies the whole learning philosophy at its finest. Individual writing and research, various content area concepts, interpersonal and oral presentation skills all come together in a natural way to yield meaningful results to individual students and the class as well.

As long as I live I will never forget the experience of one girl who at first protested the project on the grounds that "famous people won't talk to us; we're just kids." She ended up spending a day at the Brandywine River Museum, world famous home of the Wyeth paintings, as the personal guest of George Weymouth, the museum's founder and director of the Brandywine Conservancy. Obviously she learned a great deal from that experience. By sharing her experience with the group through an oral report and slide presentation, she completed the whole learning cycle for the rest of us as well.

The fifth report returned to a more typical pattern. This report concerned a topic from the history of our area. The students selected a person or event from our regional history, researched it, described it, and explained its significance to our area.

Report six combined the skills learned in the previous reports. This time the students, working in pairs, selected a township within the watershed boundaries to research. This research, however, required each pair of students to visit the township and interview a township official. This meant the students had to write another letter, set up an appointment, visit the township and conduct an interview. The final report, in addition to the written information gathered from the interview and any other research, had to include maps and photographs of the township.

Each student created a "year in review" newspaper for report number seven. Students researched events and living conditions from specific nineteenth century years. Then they wrote newspaper articles and editorials to convey what they had learned to the rest of us. By the time all forty had presented their oral reports based on their newspaper, we had a pretty good idea of what life in the 1800's must have been like around Philadelphia.

Past and present merged in report eight as students researched environmental problems which confront us in the late twentieth century. To understand these issues fully, students traced the origins of the problems, examined the current status of the problems, and predicted future solutions—or future conditions should no solution be found.

Report nine reestablished the human aspect of all our studies. Students selected an important Brandywine valley personality, from any period of time, and described that person's contribution to the quality of life locally and in terms of the larger world as well.

The final report pulled everything together. Each student wrote a "State of the Valley" report. This included elements of the watershed's geographic features, its history, its culture, its economic and demographic development, its current condition, and finally, its future.

Augmenting the ten research report projects, we fulfilled our original goal to get the students out of the building and into the real world. We took approximately twenty-five field study trips to the river that year. On each trip the students sketched, wrote descriptions or poetry, took measurements, searched for benthic invertebrates and completed chemical tests. In addition to these field study trips, the class visited the Lenni-Lenape Museum in Allentown, Pennsylvania; Fort Christina and the "Rocks" in

Wilmington, Delaware, site of the first Swedish settlement; the American-Swedish Historical Museum in Philadelphia; the Morton Homestead; the DuPont Company's early black powder yards at the Hagley Museum, also in Wilmington; the Brandywine River Museum; the Brandywine Battle-field Park; several water and waste water treatment plants, and a landfill.

We also allowed for and encouraged student ideas, since part of our philosophy asserts that the students should have a sense of ownership and control of their own education. Maintenance work on our woodstrip canoes, for example, prompted some students to decide that they wanted to build a canoe of their own. So, one student designed it, and we all helped construct the new canoe. This involved months of hard work cutting, bending, gluing and tacking together hundreds of thin strips of yellow pine over forms created by the student designer. All the labor was accomplished voluntarily during the students' self-directed time.

Another student became interested in snowshoes after reading about the Lenape. He learned to make snowshoes using branches and leather thongs. Then he taught the class how to make them. Yet another boy became enamored of the dioramas we saw at the Hagley Museum. He built his own model of an early American grist mill. Others painted murals, some in our room, some in the hallways. One of these became the basis for the logo we continue to use on our letterhead. We were amazed at the variety and complexity of the special projects students designed and implemented as were the many guests who visited.

Hans J. '88

Beyond these parts of our original plan, we imitated the Swedish colonists and improvised. Wishing to avoid the colonists' major problem—their inability to communicate with home—we established three main avenues of communication: weekly folders, monthly newsletters, and bi-monthly open house evenings.

The weekly folder consisted of a plain manila folder which contained all of the student's work for the week, a comment from us, and a list of assignments on which the student was working. Students shared the folder with their parents each week, and the parent confirmed this sharing by writing a comment and signing. This gave the parents a chance to see exactly what their children were doing, to share in that learning, and to communicate to us each week any concerns they may have had.

We have experimented over the intervening years with various comment forms and folder day logistics. For example, we have added a student self-evaluation component, and we ask the students to write a goal for the coming week in addition to their assessment of the past week. One year we tried sending folders to one quarter of the students on Mondays, to another quarter on Tuesdays, and so forth. We though this might make the comment writing easier, or at least less burdensome. In fact, we found that this procedure created an even larger bookkeeping problem, so we have returned to using Wednesday as folder day for everyone. We try as often as possible to have the students write their comments on Tuesday afternoon so we can take their comment sheets home to complete that evening. This has helped a great deal.

Nevertheless, despite these alterations, the weekly folder procedure remains an integral part of WATERSHED. Samples of past and present forms can be found in Appendix D. Informal interviews with parents reveal that this procedure for parental involvement is one of their most treasured aspects of the WATERSHED experience. Many parents openly bemoan the lack of communication they experience before and after their WATERSHED year.

...these reports are not grades. They are descriptions of each student's accomplishments, strengths, and areas needing continued work.

Parenthetically, in addition to these weekly folder comments, Ed and I write two lengthier narrative descriptions of each child's performance and progress during the year. We send these progress reviews home in January and June. Copies also go into the student's permanent record file in place of the traditional report card. Once again, these reports are not grades. They are descriptions of each student's accomplishments, strengths, and areas needing continued work.

As another medium of communication, the monthly newsletter became a student production. Each student signed up to work on at least one newsletter over the course of the year. These editorial teams design the cover, create a calendar of up-coming events, select samples of their classmates' written and artistic work, write special descriptions of the month's trips and major activities, plan and organize the layout, and then distribute the copies of their edition.

At first Ed and I made it easier for the editorial teams by saving for them particularly good drawings or pieces of writing that were handed in to us. Later we turned that job entirely over to the students. Unfortunately, during years three and four, for various reasons the students experienced difficulties gathering adequate submissions from their peers. So, in year five we began requiring each student to submit a work of his or her own choosing each month to the newsletter committee. Thus far this has proven to be the most effective method. It gives the students control over their own submissions; it gives the editors control over the final product; and it ensures that sufficient materials will be available to the committee come publication time each month.

A copy of the newsletter. appropriately titled "WATERSHED CURRENT EVENTS" goes home with each student. Remaining copies are delivered by the editors to each of our building and district administrators, our guidance counselors, our support service teachers, and a number of other teachers who simply enjoy reading what the students produce. We also keep a file anthology of all previous issues which we show to visitors, and which we take with us when we make presentations about the WATERSHED program.

Open House evenings, held every other month, are also a student responsibility. Once again, each student must serve on at least one Open House committee during the year. This committee plans the entire event. The students determine the schedule for the evening, including what demonstrations and readings will be presented, by whom, what cooperative games will be played, what slides will be shown, and what refreshments will be served. The committee members also serve as emcee/hosts for the evening's activities. This gives each student yet another opportunity to practice and sharpen public speaking skills, as well as another chance to showcase his or her accomplishments. The students love the Open House evenings.

So do the parents, and the evenings are always successful. Parental attendance generally runs close to 90%, and often the entire family will come, complete with siblings, grandparents, aunts and uncles. Obviously the parents enjoy sharing in the WATERSHED experience as much as the students love "showing off" what they have learned and accomplished. These evenings allow us to get to know the parents better under informal conditions. We get to talk with many parents individually over the course of the evening to discuss their child's progress; and we always reserve a few minutes of the evening's agenda for what the students have dubbed "the Mark and Ed Show," when we get to make general comments, announcements and invitations to the parents as a group.

Parents from the first year, when polled on various issues toward the end of that year, suggested that we hold a conference evening in lieu of an Open House at some point mid-way through the year. Parents felt a need to talk with us without the students present—an understandable concern to be sure. So, in year number two we instituted just such a conference evening. We scheduled it for January, just after the parents received our written mid-year progress review of their child's work. Conferences were optional, but virtually every parent chose to schedule and attend one. As one might expect, this proved very useful to us as well as to the parents, and we have continued the practice ever since.

During year number five, the entire school was required to hold a conference night in deference to our recently added fifth graders. Our elementary schools have always had parent conference time, and the fifth grade teachers now at the middle school rightfully wanted to continue that practice. Unfortunately, the decision was made to hold the conferences early in November, too early in the year as far as we were concerned; and we protested to that effect. Yet, we in WATERSHED were required to go along with the crowd, and it was indeed a very crowded evening. Though most of our parents once again attended this evening, we agreed to continue to offer our January conference as well so the parents could discuss the mid-year progress reviews. It is interesting to note that the school is now exploring the possibility of letting each grade level of each team schedule its own conference evening to avoid the crowds and to avoid the massive scheduling problems that arose for parents with more than one child at the middle school.

A great part of WATERSHED's success as an academic experiment can be directly attributed to parental input and cooperation.

In any case, we successfully avoided the communications problems experienced by the early Swedish settlers. A great part of WATERSHED's success as an academic experiment can be directly attributed to parental input and cooperation made possible and enhanced by the open channels of communication. Parents attended Open Houses; they accompanied us on trips; they visited the classroom. They were always welcome; they knew it, and they appreciated it.

On the last Friday of the school year, we took a family canoe trip down the Brandywine. This, too, has become a ritual part of the program, a special event that has grown in popularity each year. That first year, thirty-five canoes of students and their parents together celebrated their river, their WATERSHED experiences, and each other. Last June, we needed forty-eight canoes. After a weekend's recuperation, the parents joined us for a final Open House evening. Then they hosted an end-of-the-year party for the class on the next to last day of school.

Nothing is more crucial to a child's success than support from home, and nothing could be easier to promote. We have seen the tremendous benefits derived from just a little added effort on our part as teachers to reach out to the parents, to encourage them to become more active participants. Yet, one of the most frequent complaints we hear from alumni parents concerns their difficulty readjusting to the lack of involvement and communication once their child returns to the traditional eighth grade program. On the other side of that coin, when we talk to various school groups we often hear complaints that it is the parents in the community who are too busy or too disinterested to become involved. In either case, I believe a little added effort on the part of the schools to reach out to the community, to find convenient times for working parents through flexible scheduling for example, would yield results similar to the positive ones we experienced. Furthermore, these positive results would go a long way toward helping to solve many of the problems in today's schools.

Unfortunately, the traditional school structure, which gives each of many teachers partial responsibility for over one hundred students severely restricts the potential for effective, positive, and on-going communications between parents and teachers. Thus, once again the WATERSHED approach with its emphasis on regrouping for smaller whole learning classes encourages and allows far greater parental participation to occur. Better communications might well have saved the New Sweden colony; it could certainly help save public education in America. Ⱳ

Canoeing builds cooperation skills and a sense of community.
It also provides great experiences to write about.

Growth and Changes 4.

The lack of communication with and support from home hampered the growth of the New Sweden colony from the very beginning. Young Queen Christina's eyes turned to heavenly rather than earthly concerns. As a result, the venture suffered during its earliest years deprivations befitting martyrdom.

Fortunately, the Lenape proved friendly—perhaps because the Swedish sauna appeared to the Lenape to match their own ceremonial sweat lodge; or perhaps because the twenty-four blond settlers were not sufficiently numerous to pose a serious threat to the hundreds of Lenape living in the region. Whatever the reason, the Lenape saved the colony that first year. They taught the Swedes and Finns to grow corn and tobacco. They provided the colonists with furs and meat from their own hunting and trapping forays when the Swedes were not successful with theirs.

Meanwhile, no help came from Sweden.

To further complicate matters, Minuit was gone. He had sailed the *Kalmar Nyckel* to the West Indies as soon as the fort had been built and armed. There he died, lost at sea aboard a Dutch ship during an unexpectedly severe storm.

He had left his ship to dine with a friend, the captain of a Dutch ship anchored in the same port. When the weather worsened suddenly, both ships put out to sea for safety.

The *Kalmar Nyckel* survived. The Dutch vessel and Peter Minuit vanished. The *Kalmar Nyckel* continued her voyage back to Sweden, but it would be almost two full years before she returned to Fort Christina with fresh supplies, settlers, and news of home.

In that time, the settlers relied heavily on the Lenape. Many men learned the Lenape language, and some probably took Lenape wives. In any case, evidence indicates that these Swedes and Finns got along exceedingly well with the Lenape, and much better than did the Dutch further up the Delaware valley. We note, for example, that the Lenape and their Minquas overlords preferred to trade with the Swedes. Perhaps because the Swedes gave more in trade for the furs, or perhaps because the Swedes' location on the west side of the Delaware River made them more accessible; the native trappers soon gave much more of their business to the Swedes than to the Dutch across the river.

The Dutch were quick to complain, both to the new settlers and to the Swedish crown. As you can imagine, their complaints fell on deaf ears on both sides of the Atlantic. Not wanting to provoke the greater Swedish military might in Europe, the Dutch restricted their New World hostilities to letters of protest.

In the meantime, Fort Christina developed slowly on its own. America's first log cabins, later to become the very symbol of the American frontier experience, were built along the banks of the Christina, the Brandywine, and the Delaware Rivers. A sauna and a log church were erected along with the fort. Forests gave way to small fields of tobacco—the only cash crop grown—and corn. Sheep grazed and multiplied on the hillsides of the fall line. The *Fogel Grip* sailed to Virginia to establish trade with the English, but the English refused to let her dock. As far as the English were concerned, they owned the entire east coast of North America, and these Swedes had no business being there.

"Swedish Log Cabin at Fort Christina Park" drawing by Cynthia Galli '93

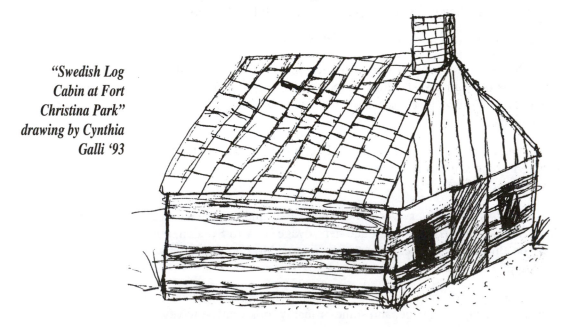

The Fogel Grip returned to Fort Christina; and the settlers, with the help of the Lenape, were forced to fend for themselves.

Eventually, the *Kalmar Nyckel* returned, followed sporadically by other ships over the next few years. However, they brought with them too few new settlers and too few supplies to replenish adequately New Sweden's dwindling stores. The ships returned to Sweden with minimal and decreasing gains in furs and tobacco. New Sweden existed on the edge of a new world and on the edge of extinction.

Then, in 1642, Queen Christina saw fit to send a new royal governor to the floundering colony.

Given his mixed military record, Johan Printz could never be sure whether his new commission was a promotion or a demotion. Yet, he determined to make the most of the situation and to make a name for himself in the New World. "Big Belly," as the Lenape appropriately named the three hundred pound Printz, arrived in New Sweden in 1643 with as much pomp as circumstances would allow. He surveyed the rude community of log cabins and quickly set about making changes.

To begin with, he moved his colonial government from Fort Christina up the Delaware River to Tinicum Island, near the present site of the Philadelphia International Airport. There he built a new fort and a two story house for himself, complete with glass windows. Then he set about to fulfill his royal instructions. Neither his authoritarian attitude nor his glass windows went over particularly well with the colonists.

As WATERSHED's second year began, we, too, welcomed a new "governor." Our principal and mentor, Anne Janson, who had been so instrumental in launching WATERSHED, moved to the central administration building next door to RMS to become the Assistant Superintendent in charge of personnel. A new principal assumed command. As one of his first duties, this new principal had instructions to review our pilot WATERSHED program and submit a full report to the Board. Though we were promised a two-year pilot, staffing decisions for the third year

"Big Belly"
(Johan Printz)
Elizabeth Maddox '91

had to be made by the spring of the second. Since the existence of WATERSHED certainly impacted on staffing needs, the report that would determine the continuation of the program had to be submitted by December of 1988. So, in essence, we had to describe and evaluate the pilot on the basis of just one year's experience. While this was hardly optimal from our point of view, it was understandable and unavoidable. So, we sat down to determine a procedure to complete the evaluation.

After several meetings with our new principal, we decided the evaluation report would consist of four main sections:

— a description of the program, its philosophy, its goals, and the implemental strategies employed in the first year;
— a program cost analysis with comparisons to traditional program expenses;
— data concerning the students' academic performance, including standardized test results, grade level writing sample results, and preliminary eighth grade evaluations;
— data concerning affective evaluation by the students, the parents and other interested parties.

The first section seemed straightforward enough when the principal proposed it. We gathered copies of our original proposal which contained our philosophy and our goal statements. We collated examples of the ten report assignment sheets, and we prepared to describe the major trips and activities in which the students had participated. Easy enough.

Then our principal brought out his glass windows: he asked us "to divide the assignments and activities by subject areas." Whether he realized it or not, he was asking for the antithesis of everything WATERSHED stood for, of everything we had wanted to achieve when we designed and proposed the program. He was asking us, at least symbolically, to undo all the work we had done setting up and implementing the program, to break apart the very connections we had labored to build, and to reconstruct the very walls between the so-called disciplines we had sought to destroy.

I must admit, from the traditional point of view, this request represented a logical point of view, and it remains a widespread problem for us. When Ed and I travel to talk about the program, we emphasize the integrated, whole learning nature of the process involved. After all, this is the very heart of the WATERSHED approach. We present numerous examples of the activities we employ to blend the disciplines back together and to refocus the students' attentions onto the interrelatedness of knowledge. Yet, after we go through our presentation, we almost always have someone in the audience ask questions such as "When do the students do English?" or "When do they do art?" Many educators experience tremendous difficulty seeing beyond the limiting confines of their training. Hence this book: one more attempt to show a different methodology to what is largely conservative profession.

Be that as it may, we faced this task of providing traditional descriptions for a non-traditional program. In a sense, we had to describe our round-peg program as if it possessed parallel sides in order to make it look like it would fit into someone else's definition of a particular space.

Never ones to take a challenge lightly, we listed every major activity, assignment, guest speaker, and field trip. Then we categorized them by student product and date with their "subject area emphases," and did it again with reference to "thinking skills emphases," and yet a third time with respect to "communications skills emphases." The resultant thirty pages of lists, though meaningless from our point of view, ironically proved extremely effective and set a new standard for other departmental reviews.

If nothing else, however, these lists served to prove that WATERSHED is not the Sixty-ish, fluff program some staff members said it would be. Nor is it the New Age mystical experience some people assume it to be when we speak of holistic learning. The number of written assignments alone demonstrated the high degree of academic rigor involved—and proved as well that students in WATERSHED do in fact "do English."

The number of written assignments alone demonstrated the high degree of academic rigor involved.

Another myth was dispelled when the cost comparison section was completed by the principal himself.

Since WATERSHED is a highly visible program with its numerous excursions and frequent publicity releases, many non-participant members of the community assumed that WATERSHED costs more than other programs. In fact, some particularly vocal parents complained that WATERSHED students were receiving more of the local tax dollars than were their own children.

WATERSHED was, and is, cost effective.

To the amazement and embarrassment of many, WATERSHED proved to be less expensive per pupil than the regular program. True, we have transportation expenses for all our field trips—expenses which, by the way, have decreased dramatically since we shifted in year four to more van trips and fewer bus trips. However, we required no textbook expenditures (though a potential figure was even inserted into the WATERSHED calculation), very little in the way of supplies, and significantly fewer teacher salary dollars per pupil contact time. WATERSHED clearly was, and is, cost effective. To this day our total budget is smaller than most individual department budgets, and our per pupil costs remain lower than that of other, more traditional teams.

WATERSHED students performed on a par with the control students in math, but significantly better than the control group in reading.

For the data concerning academic performance, we turned to our guidance department. They gathered information from a variety of sources, starting with our reading specialist, Patty Lee. Referring to reading test results for WATERSHED students, Patty reported, "...test scores and class work reflect growth in reading at or beyond expectation..." for five of the fourteen WATERSHED students who had been recommended to have special reading instruction during seventh grade. Six of the fourteen "maintained" expected levels. Three "...all of whom showed marked reading deficiencies prior to enrollment in the WATERSHED program have shown remarkable progress." In fact, they showed "....evidence of one to two years' growth in reading." Keep in mind, because they elected to be in WATERSHED, these same students did *not* participate in the reading program for which they had been recommended.

These early, first year findings were substantiated several years later in a 1994 study conducted by Robert Hassler (1994) as part of his doctoral thesis at Lehigh University. Mr. Hassler, working independently, compared various testing scores and survey results from WATERSHED students and a control group including the both of our two other more traditional seventh grade teams. He concluded that WATERSHED students performed on a par with the control students in math, but significantly better than the control group in reading. With respect to the attitudinal surveys, Mr. Hassler found that WATERSHED students exhibited the same pattern of shifting attitudes that all seventh graders show. From this Mr. Hassler concluded that "educators may develop alternative methods of curriculum design similar to those in this study without apprehension of negative results."

Standardized test scores analyzed by our own guidance department in 1988 showed no significant difference between WATERSHED and non-WATERSHED seventh graders. While this may at first appear to cast some doubt on the academic value of WATERSHED's whole learning approach, keep in mind that the standardized tests are predicated on conventional content and strategies of instruction. For us to emphasize nonconventional content and employ radically different strategies while still maintaining a similar degree of success in the standardized test scores actually supports the validity of the whole learning approach. Were the roles reversed; were we somehow to create a "standardized test" based on WATERSHED's content and methods, one wonders if students from traditional programs would succeed equally well.

The most telling evidence of academic success, however, came in the form of the seventh grade writing sample. Every September the entire seventh grade was required to write a timed essay on a topic determined by the English department. Each student received a number which he or she put at the top of the paper in lieu of a name. This way the papers would be anonymous as far as the evaluators were concerned, but the classroom teachers kept a record correlating names and numbers so final results could be analyzed and appropriate instructional steps taken.

The essays were then collected and scored holistically by members of the English department. Two teachers read each essay and gave it a score of one to four, four being the best. If a difference of opinion occurred, a third teacher read the essay and decided the final score. It is important to emphasize that the evaluators did not know the identities of the students and thus did not know whether a student was in WATERSHED or the regular program. It is equally important to note that neither Ed nor I was involved in the scoring process at all.

This procedure was then repeated in the spring and the results compared. The theory held that keeping the same score from autumn to spring represented a normal year's growth and progress. Any upward change in the score would indicate accelerated improvement. Pre and post papers were collated by their number and returned to the classroom teachers.

The results proved quite remarkable. Fifteen of our forty WATER-SHED students received improved scores on their post-test. That amounts to 37.5% of our group showing marked improvement. Taken as a whole, the entire seventh grade showed a much smaller percentage of improved scores. Furthermore, when one looked at the raw data, our fifteen students with improved scores accounted for almost the entire number of students in seventh grade who received better scores. Clearly something noteworthy was happening with respect to writing in WATERSHED.

In all fairness, it must be noted that these results are not due to the superior teaching abilities on the part of the WATERSHED teachers; nor , for that matter, is it due to any lack of superior teaching abilities on the part of the traditional English staff. Rather, I contend that the improved writing scores result directly from the superiority of the whole learning methodology.

... writing assignments involve topics relevant to the students and the rest of their curricular experiences.

First, the WATERSHED approach provides consistency. We see everything the student writes. Second, the writing assignments given in WATERSHED involve topics more relevant to the students and to the rest of the students' curricular experiences. In many English classes, isolated as most are from the other subject areas, assignments are somewhat arbitrary and lacking in direct connection to the students' experiences, personal or curricular. Third, the WATERSHED time schedule allows the

teachers involved the opportunity to work more closely with each individual child. We get to know the student. We have the time to see where problems exist and then to work individually with the student to correct the problems. The teacher in a regular English classroom who has to deal with one hundred or more students each day in forty minute time blocks never has an adequate opportunity to work closely with the students. Nor does that teacher with the large class load have time to spend reading papers.

So, it is clearly not a matter of teachers' abilities in this case, but rather the superiority of the teaching situation which enhances growth in students' writing abilities: yet another argument for radically restructuring the traditional school scheduling practices, particularly in middle level education.

The final section of the pilot evaluation, and my personal favorite, included the student and parent responses to exit questionnaires, comments from student self-evaluations, unsolicited letters from parents and others who visited the program during the year, and copies of various newspaper articles written about the program. It also included two poems written by students and presented to us at the year's end. Taken together, this evidence clearly showed the value the students and their parents placed on the WATERSHED experience.

Taken as a whole, the one hundred page report convinced the School Board to make WATERSHED an ongoing part of the Radnor Middle School program of studies. And so we continue to this day.

Just for the record, we made a revised presentation to the School Board in the spring of 1993. The Board by then consisted almost entirely of people who had not been part of the Board in 1988. They asked many of the same questions the previous board had asked. Apparently, this Board was as satisfied with the responses as the previous Board had been.

Like the early Swedish settlers, however, WATERSHED existed through its earliest years without much more support from the educational establishment. I find it remarkable that, in light of the program's obvious success, popularity, and economic feasibility, the only serious efforts to duplicate the whole learning process are occurring in other districts.

The significant point for now, however, is that unlike that Swedish colony, WATERSHED does continue to exist. Printz's ten year reign, rocky and turbulent as it was, solidified the Swedish colonial effort. Printz expanded the colony in all directions except to the east, improved trade and the cultivation of tobacco, and kept the Dutch competitors at bay through cunning and bravado.

Unfortunately, Printz's successor, Johan Rising, lacked Printz's managerial and military savvy. To maintain control of the Delaware Bay, Rising captured a Dutch fort at Casimir, south of Fort Christina. This proved one move too many for the Dutch governor of New Amsterdam, Peter Stuyvesant. Stuyvesant dispatched several warships from New Amsterdam, and the New Sweden colony surrendered without a shot. By this time, 1655, Queen Christina had all but abandoned any concern for her fledgling colony. She, too, gave up without a fight.

And so New Sweden became part of New Amsterdam, but only until 1664, when the entire area became the property of the English crown.

For our part, despite the lack of support for expansion, and despite the difficulties involved in the pilot evaluation process, the WATERSHED program continued to develop. The students in year number two proved to be just as enthusiastic and committed to the vision as their predecessors. In fact, perhaps because they knew the fate of the program was not clear at that time, they seemed to strive with added vigor to prove that the alternative approach worked better than its conventional counterpart. Perhaps, as some have admitted, because they did not share in what they saw as the honor of being the very first WATERSHED group, they pulled together to ensure that they would not be the last. In that process, the group of very disparate individuals formed a unique bond and a special identity of their own.

Once again we employed the same basic research report structure that we had used in year one. We did make some minor refinements, however, to make the pieces fit together more smoothly. Most notable among these, we tied the topographical map work to the township report. Instead of assigning each student a random square of the watershed to make for the three dimensional map, we paired the students early on so they could make map sections of the same township they eventually studied for report number six.

The trip schedule and the guest speakers continued, with several notable additions. Students were able to host talks by noted authorities on Lenape culture and Quaker history, for example. In the case of the former, our guest, from a local university, shared new research that made obsolete much of what we had previously learned about the Lenape. Our Quaker historian brought with him numerous artifacts, deeds, and stories from his personal history which touched many aspects of our study. For example, he had with him a small cannonball from the Battle of the Brandywine. This particular cannonball had been found in a tree stump on the Kuerner farm in Chaddsford, Pennsylvania. That very same tree stump can be seen in Andrew Wyeth's painting, "Ground Hog Day," which was painted shortly after the tree was chopped down and the cannonball found. Our guest, a

Interpretation of Andrew Wyeth's 'Ground Hog Day' drawing by B.J. Hetrick '94

friend of both the Kuerners and the Wyeths, had been present at that time and was given the cannonball. History, culture, and personal narrative came together in a magical moment for the WATERSHED students.

The most significant of the new trips was the canoe trip to begin the year. It gave the students a chance to form their group identity by sharing a unique experience. This trip, done without parents, was both successful and popular; so, it, too, has become a WATERSHED tradition.

We also added a community service project involving a week-long series of five visits to the Brandywine Valley Association's Myrick Center. There the students designed and constructed from the foundation up a small greenhouse. This greenhouse captured and used the gray water from the center's sinks. Thus, the project involved community service, design and construction components, and the investigation and understanding of waste water treatment procedures. It also involved a great deal of fun, to say nothing of the tremendous sense of accomplishment the students all felt when the project was finished.

Furthermore, the week involved many other learning experiences as well as those associated with the greenhouse itself. Since all thirty-six students could not possibly work on the small structure at the same time, we divided the class into five work details. While one of these work details labored on the greenhouse, another did water testing in the nearby Brandywine, a third group practiced orienteering and visited a stream seep on BVA property, another group did clean up and conservation work around the Myrick Center, and the final group took a bus tour to visit numerous monuments, markers, and Friends' meetinghouses in the area. We rotated activities daily so all students enjoyed each of the five experiences.

Once again, this procedure worked so well that we repeated it in year three, our last year focusing on the Brandywine. BVA did not need another greenhouse, however, so the third year's WATERSHED class built a puppet theater and made puppets for the BVA education center.

Another magical moment occurred during that greenhouse week at BVA. While doing conservation work along one of the many trails on the BVA property, one of our students unearthed a small cannonball identical to the one we had been shown by our guest speaker just a few weeks earlier. For that young lady, and for the rest of us as well, history became a truly personalized experience!

In addition to additional guest speakers and the new trips, the second year also included a new group project back in the classroom. As the municipalities in Pennsylvania faced the onset of mandatory recycling, we had the students form recycling companies to devise workable plans for township recycling programs. The students had to decide which materials to recycle, how to collect those materials, what to do with the collected materials, where to locate recycling facilities and industries, how much it would cost or save the township, and how to educate the local citizenry and promote the recycling program. Then the students had to "sell" their company's plan to a hypothetical township board of directors, namely the rest of the class.

To say the groups did a fantastic job does not even begin to do them the justice they deserve. They dug up information from the library; they contacted township supervisors and existing recycling companies; they asked the right questions, developed new ideas, and finally made presentations that could rival those the real township board heard from the professionals. In fact, I think some of the plans that the students developed made more sense environmentally and economically that did the plan which became reality in Radnor Township.

With all this, the students still found time to conduct their stream testing trips, to make their three-dimensional map of the Brandywine, to do research and write their reports. They produced monthly newsletters and a wonderful year-end anthology of writing and artwork. They hosted five Open House evenings; they finished fiberglassing the canoe started by the first year's group; they painted more murals; they made a large model of the chemical structures involved in photosynthesis; and they built several scale model canoes. If anything, despite the distractions of the pilot evaluation, year two proved to be even more productive that the first year had been.

At the close of that first year, Ed and I had been touched by the students' fairly universal desire to stay in school after that final bell had rung signaling the onset of summer vacation. The second year's group remained in their last sharing circle, many in tears, even as the other students in the school made their traditionally raucous exit. These WATERSHED students simply did not want their year to end. ⧢

The Brandywine near Pocopson Bridge

No Cross, No Crown, No Names Above the Door

5.

By the year 1672, when George Fox traveled through this region on his way from Quaker meetings in Maryland to meetings in New England, the earliest Swedish and Dutch settlers were well mixed and assimilated into a small, general population. Few towns per se as yet existed. Fox traveled from house to house, staying some nights in snug Swedish log cabins, sleeping other nights in drafty wattle and daub English homes.

Regardless of the accommodations, Fox was obviously impressed with this area just west of the Delaware River. When he returned to England in 1673, one of the first people with whom he spoke was a young man by the name of William Penn. Fox told Penn of this relatively unpopulated area in the New World which contained the promise of excellence in its rich soils and verdant forests. One can almost imagine the two Quakers discussing their shared dreams of establishing a place where their Religious Society of Friends could truly be free to worship according to their consciences.

Within a decade, their dreams became a reality.

King Charles II, and his younger brother James, then the Duke of York, were good friends of the Penn family. Despite their religious differences, or maybe because of those differences, the two families maintained an easy alliance.

Penn's father served the Stuarts as General of the Seas, and the Stuarts owed Penn's father a considerable amount of back pay at the time of the admiral's death. More significant, perhaps, the Stuarts had also promised Admiral Penn that they would "look after" the younger Penn, whose Quaker convictions had already gotten him thrown out of Oxford and thrown into jail.

At precisely what point it happened, I am not sure; but somewhere along the line King Charles had a brilliant idea. He would repay his debt to the Admiral by giving William, Jr. some land in the Americas. William could move there along with many of his Friends, thus sparing the crown a great deal of trouble on two counts. First, the King would not have to keep rescuing young William from the Tower of London. Second, the King would not have to deal so often with the religious difficulties presented by the existence of the dissident Quakers.

Just who suggested the idea, I again cannot say; but a large tract of land west of the Delaware River was deeded over to William Penn. Penn wanted to name his new colony "Sylvania" after the vast forests George Fox had described to him. To this the King asked to prefix the name Penn. In true Quaker fashion, William objected. To name a colony after himself, Penn argued, would surely be a vanity. I wonder how long the King let young William chew upon his own foot before informing William that the Penn being so honored was the Admiral, not the son. At any rate, "Pennsylvania" became a reality.

And so William Penn set out to people his new colony and to assure those already living in the region that his intentions as proprietor differed significantly from what they might suspect.

To understand this, one has to understand a little of Penn's Quaker beliefs. Without going into lengthy detail, suffice it to say that to the Friends all people share equally in the glory and spirit of God. In this sense, the Quakers believed much as did the Lenape, though with a monotheistic rather than pantheistic definition of God. Enlightened conscience was more important than creeds, classes, or crowns; and every person, regardless of creed, class, or crown had the capacity for enlightened conscience. Furthermore, every individual deserved the right to be trusted with the responsibility for the quality of his or her own life.

This is a huge responsibility, and granting it is difficult for many even today. Yet Penn believed strongly in peoples' rights of self-determination. Furthermore, he saw the hypocrisy and the tyranny in governments and religions which denied the worth of the individual.

Indeed, it was for this very reason that Penn had been expelled from Oxford. He refused to attend mandatory chapel services with students who felt their church attendance alone absolved them of their responsibility to act morally the rest of the week. Similarly, he had been thrown into prison for writing a book entitled *No Cross, No Crown* which preached against a government and a social structure which placed class distinctions above human dignity.

Thus, when given the opportunity, Penn established his First Frame of Government for Pennsylvania. This document entitled the colonists to free-doms of religion, speech, and press. It further granted them a degree of participation in their government that was unheard of in most of the other colonies. In short, it affirmed the peoples' right to individual self-determi-nation. In many ways, Penn's beliefs served as a model for the American Constitution and the Bill of Rights to be penned some one hundred years later.

Similarly, in letters addressed to the Lenape sachems and to Swedish and Dutch inhabitants, Penn professed that they would be fairly and equally treated. He backed up his promises by enacting regulations requiring the equitable treatment of the Lenape and allowing the Swedes and the Dutch to maintain ownership of their existing homesteads. To further the cause of friendship with the Lenape, Penn learned their language, met frequently with them, and made many treaties to repurchase lands directly from them. The Lenape nicknamed him "Onas," which means quill—a fitting name for a man called Penn and for a man who signed so many treaties with a quill-pen.

At any rate, Penn's ideas quickly took hold. Welsh Quakers poured into the new colony. Philadelphia, Penn's "greene countrie towne," grew rapidly into a full-fledged city. In fact, in less than one hundred years Philadelphia grew to be the largest city in North America and second only to London, itself, as the largest English speaking city in the world.

I would like to say that WATERSHED experienced the same type of meteoric growth. I can't. I can say, however, that we created an educa-tional microcosm based on the same general principles concerning the rights and responsibilities of the individual. For example, each student and his or her parents are asked to read and sign a statement describing their respec-tive responsibilities. While a complete copy of this statement can be found in Appendix E, suffice it here to say that the participants are expected to take responsibility for their own actions and to act at all times in accor-dance with WATERSHED's five basic tenets:

Commitment,

Cooperation,

Courage,

Caution,

Caring.

Every year, on the first day of school, the WATERSHED students enter the only classroom in Radnor Middle School that does not have any teacher's name stamped above it. The students' first task: draft their own set of rules and expectations. We post this list prominently in the classroom, and we refer to it frequently throughout the year. The day-to-day classroom activities are similarly designed to give the students as many opportunities as possible to determine their own behavior and to take responsibility for their time. Ed and I spend as little time as possible in front of the entire group "lecturing." We prefer to devote our time to discussion sessions and project work, some of which is organized by groups, some by individuals. In either case, this allows the students the freedom to select when and for how long they want to work on a particular task. It also makes them directly responsible for the time allotted and their results. Do they always rise to the occasion? Of course not; but that's what the learning experience is all about.

This set of principles adapted to the public school milieu sets WATERSHED apart from traditional educational practices and makes it a model for education in the 21st century. I realize how grandiose that sounds, but I am confident that it is true nonetheless.

Few would deny that the present educational structure in this country grew out of nineteenth century conditions when massive numbers of immigrant workers had to be trained, for the first time in human history, to perform tasks that required rudimentary skills in reading, writing, and arithmetic. Yet, at that same time, the majority of these masses also had to be trained to believe themselves satisfied with routine, repetitive jobs on factory assembly lines and in shuffle-paper offices. Teach people, but do not let them think too much. Public education was created, at least in large part, to fill this socioeconomic need.

Thus the new educational system took children off the streets and out of the fields and put them in straight rows of cramped desks; conditions which paralleled the working conditions many would face in factory sweatshops. Schools disciplined children to sit quietly for long periods of time, to obey the commands of authority without question, and to memorize the basics of communicating and counting—at least enough to satisfy the needs of the workplace and to read the advertisements which would prompt them to buy the goods produced.

For a while, this was indeed an advancement. People who would have remained illiterate in bygone eras learned to read and write, and the economy grew. The two went hand-in-hand to everyone's apparent advantage. A high school diploma—earned for time served with good behavior—became one's meal ticket, one's entry pass into a life at least materialistically superior to that of one's parents. We note, however, that for quite a long time the society continued to reserve a college education for the elite; for those wealthy enough to afford it, those predestined to assume their fathers' roles in the corporate headquarters, or for those fortunate few who showed enough promise or good fortune to be admitted to that inner circle.

Inside the schools, the assembly line became the model of choice. Complex knowledge was splintered into simpler, seemingly discrete segments. These segments, appropriately called "disciplines," could be presented in manageable time blocks. Memorized "mastery" could supposedly be quantified and documented, much as one kept track of goods bought, sold, and stored during an inventory. Ideally, these subjects yielded a complete education if and when the student completed the compulsory twelve years.

In many ways, the structure worked amazingly well. It worked so well, in fact, that it outmoded itself by the middle of the twentieth century. Unfortunately, by that time the structure had so ingrained itself into the fiber of our culture that it had taken on a life of its own. A complete self-fulfilling hierarchy had arisen. Elementary schools "prepared" students for junior high schools. Junior high schools "prepared" students for high schools. High schools "prepared" students for the increasing number of colleges. Colleges "prepared" students to go on to graduate or professional schools, or to go back to the beginning and become teachers. Teaching for the real world of integrated knowledge virtually disappeared.

Ironically, in order to preserve itself, the system was forced to push more and more people up through higher and higher levels. The high school diploma, once a status symbol and meal ticket, was devalued by an inflationary educational system. Those hitherto excluded from the latter stages of the system began to demand access to it—in order to obtain a "better" job, not to get a better education, per se.

Almost symbiotically, certainly simultaneously, the workplace changed from a manufacturing base to a service base and then, more recently, to an information base. The very nature of most work changed from routine assembly line repetitions to increasingly more sophisticated tasks requiring higher and higher levels of thinking skills and greater and greater degrees of integrated knowledge.

To this point, all worked quite nicely; but here the system broke down. As the needs of the workplace changed and the workers within it became increasingly sophisticated, the educational system should have adjusted itself. Conditions and clientele had changed significantly. Yet, the educational system remained virtually unchanged. In fact, the established structure vehemently resisted change. As we approach the 21st century, our schools still reflect the factory image of a century ago in terms of physical plant, curricular structure, and the attitude toward the role of the individual learner.

As we approach the 21st century, our schools still reflect the factory image of a century ago in terms of physical plant, curricular structure, and the attitude toward the role of the individual learner.

Much has been made lately of the obvious failure of our schools to meet the needs of our changing society. Unfortunately, too many critics of the system fall prey to the temptation to look backward for answers rather than ahead. Even many professional educators have asserted that salvation can only be found by retreating to the simpler strategies and structures that used to work so well. More of the same, however, is necessarily doomed to failure.

Revolutionary changes in the fundamental system are necessary. In a world where information, a.k.a. "facts," is transmitted and changes literally at the speed of light, students must learn to handle information, not memorize it. Students must be taught how to work with ever-changing facts: how to analyze information, synthesize conclusions, reevaluate and revise on an on-going basis. Students need to work with problem solving procedures in open-ended conditions which more closely approximate the realities of the working/living world.

I would contend that one reason why so many students dislike school is their innate awareness of its false structure. They intuitively realize that school experiences bear little or no resemblance to their experiences outside school. In school, most activities seem arbitrary and disconnected. Very little seems to interrelate; information seems purposeless, and tasks have no recognizable significance beyond the fact that some teacher is requiring them. Conversely, many students enjoy sports—in fact, some endure the boring school day just to be eligible to participate in the after school sports programs. In large measure, this is because winning a game requires skills more closely aligned with real world experiences; skills in problem solving, in dealing with rapidly changing situations, and in cooperative planning and execution procedures designed to achieve a shared and meaningful goal.

Yet realistic problem-solving techniques cannot be realistically explored in the vacuum of the disciplines as they are usually taught. Integration, or whole learning, is required, particularly on primary and secondary levels. By definition, this in turn requires a restructuring of our schools away from splintered disciplines and away from time-clock schedules. It also requires that we give the individual student greater control over his or her own learning. The students ought to be involved much more directly in the planning and the implementation of their course of studies, with teachers as mentors and guides, not as line foremen.

WATERSHED offers just such a new structure. In form and content, philosophy and practice, WATERSHED embodies a whole learning approach to education. Students study significant topics, or central themes, which transcend the limits of the disciplines. Work is seen as cooperative: everyone's efforts are important to the overall success of the group as well as that of the individuals. All the content and every activity fits into a recognizable scheme based on the central theme. The student sees the interrelationship of the sub-topics and activities. Thus the students see the relevance, the need to learn these various sub-topics, not as unattached, useless ends in themselves, but as necessary means to a greater end. Finally, the learning environment places the responsibility for learning squarely on the students' shoulders where it truly belongs. Without the impending threat of grades, and with the time provided for experimentation, research, and sharing ideas, success is encouraged and failure de-emphasized.

The students are given the chance to see themselves as a part of their work and their work as part of a larger whole. The class takes on much the same aura as that of a sports team or of the cast for a play. This promotes both self-esteem and an enthusiasm for learning which the factory approach, with its generally dehumanizing strategies, cannot.

WATERSHED offers students the chance to direct their own learning in a supportive, collegial atmosphere of free speech and genuine respect for each individual. The whole learning approach encourages students to assume responsibility for their own actions, to evaluate themselves, to strive for their very best, and to look for the best in those around them. After all, if you look for the best, you are more likely to find it.

Idealistic? Of course it is. So was William Penn's "Holy Experiment," his dream of a colony with true religious freedom; a colony where people of good conscience could live freely and peacefully together, despite their differences, abiding by rules of their own making simply because they chose to do so.

Will it work?

It already has.

Work both in and out of the classroom is cooperative

Our third year saw few differences from year number two, at least in terms of projects, trips, and speakers. We focused our study on the Brandywine for the third and final time. We kept those same basic report structures, though we modified some of them slightly. The students kept logs as before, and they wrote the same types of essays and stories over the course of the year.

However, year three did witness a major difference in terms of the students. For one thing, these students were the first to have never known the Middle School without a WATERSHED program. They were also the first group to participate in the program now free from the overhanging threat of cancellation.

These students were also an extremely disparate group of individuals. Among other issues, we quickly discovered that we had in our group a pair of students who had a long and violent history of feuding with each other. Between them, they had spent more time in the disciplinarian's office the year before than they had probably spent in any particular class. We also had others who came to the group with milder but significant biases and predetermined alliances and enmities. Some of the students even experienced behavioral problems at home and in the community-at-large; problems which had nothing to do with school, itself, but which certainly effected our life in the WATERSHED room. Throughout the first half of the year, a significant part of the group devoted an extraordinary amount of time and energy (theirs as well as ours) to working through their inter-personal difficulties.

The remainder of the group, however, continued to excel. They painted more murals until we ran out of wall space. Then they started to paint murals on the windows, designing pictures which could be viewed from both inside and out—not an easy task. The class spent its week at BVA building a puppet theater and writing puppet plays about the environment for elementary school audiences. The students made puppets and scenery for these plays as well, performed the plays once for each other, then donated all the materials to BVA's education center.

Instead of a recycling company, since Radnor now had its mandatory recycling program in place, this year's group formed development companies. They were "given" a 625 acre tract of land in a rural section of the Brandywine watershed for which each company had to plan a viable new community. As a class, we visited the actual tract of land, and the students got to see what it really looked like—at that time an area of forested hillsides and rolling pastures still well away from neighboring developments.

Plans had to account for systems for waste recycling, removal, and disposal, for regional access and transportation, for public safety, for recreation and open space, and for minimal environmental disruption from potential problems such as run-off into the major streams in that area. After several weeks of research and planning, each company then presented its plan to the hypothetical zoning board consisting of the teachers and the rest of the class.

As with the previous groups' recycling plans, the ideas presented by most of these groups were outstanding and innovative. Once again, students proved that there is still hope for the future. One group in particular expressed a certain sense of disappointment when the project was over. When asked why, the group reported that they liked their plans so much, they wanted to live there!

Through these group projects and all our other shared experiences, little by little, attitudes changed. At our final sharing circle on the last day of school, the students read to each other statements each had written to express how he or she felt about the year and the group. Since their words are far more eloquent than mine, I would like to share just a few examples with you.

> *Wow! Have we changed! We've gone from slimy caterpillars to beautiful, glowing butterflies. We aren't afraid of leeches anymore, or of having to swim in deep parts of the river. We are all a family...*

> *In the beginning of the year we were the Watershed: 36 kids randomly selected by a computer. Now we are the Watershed: a family of 36 who love and care for each other. We have come a long way together, we have accomplished many things together, and we have made progress together. As the year comes to an end, I can feel a strong bond between all of us, a bond that will never be broken.*

> *In the beginning of the year no one really knew everyone. We didn't know how to work as a team, and we didn't know what the year would bring. Through the year we grew up, becoming closer as a family and becoming aware*

of each other as individuals and as a family. Over this year we have learned to care and to work as a team. I'll never forget any of you, what I learned, or what we have all learned together. I love you all...

———————————

I think we, as a group, have come a long way since September. We have tried and pushed each other to become better people. But now as a family, it will never be the same without anyone of you. Now that we are being separated, it seems that everything will fall apart. But I know if we all work and care enough, our hearts will hold on to what we've got and will never let go.

———————————

...On the first day I looked around the giant circle and thought, 'I'm going to spend the entire school year with THEM?' But everything has changed. We've all accepted everyone as equals. Together we swamped through swamps, tramped through mud, and walked hand-in-hand in cool, sometimes freezing water. We've all learned to work together be it in testing groups or development groups. We've all matured, so thank you all for everything.

———————————

I could go on and on with similar quotes, all heartfelt examples of the students' sentiments. Clearly a change had occurred, and I believe William Penn would be pleased to see his beliefs alive and well in his colony three hundred years after its inception. **W**

New Frontiers

6.

After the third year of WATERSHED, we packed up and moved to an altogether new camp. Much as the Lenape were eventually forced to leave their land under the mounting pressures of the Swedish, Dutch, and English settlers, we were forced to move to accommodate the arrival of the fifth grade to our building.

The imminent arrival of the fifth graders meant that we would all be cramped for space, as we had been back in the mid-1970s, before declining enrollments cut our middle school population in half. Enrollments are steadily rising again, but, ironically, in the intervening years our district sold off two of its four elementary school buildings and demolished a third building which had been an important portion of the middle school campus. By the late 1980s, the two remaining elementary buildings bulged with increasing numbers of little kindergarten through fifth graders. Something had to give, and the middle school was chosen.

For a little while, it actually looked as if we at the middle school might benefit from this change. It was decided that along with the fifth graders would come the concept of teaming. Though this constituted a thinly-veiled attempt to make a financial decision look like an educational decision, we in WATERSHED welcomed the concept. To this point, we were the only team in town. An expert from a nearby university was hired as a consultant, the staff underwent more in-service days, and ideas for teaming were explored.

Truly this seemed a golden opportunity to expand the WATERSHED concept. After all, everything the consultant advised for staff and students alike could be achieved through the implementation of more WATERSHED-like, whole learning teams. Seventh graders, we were told for example, need a place to belong, not an impersonal mosaic schedule. These active adolescents need an environment that allows movement and encourages exploratory and cooperative learning. Twelve and thirteen year olds require multi-sensory stimuli learning and a greater variety of ways to demonstrate mastery of materials and concepts. I could go on and on listing the special needs of the middle level child in today's educational system—needs which the WATERSHED program's whole learning approach was specifically designed to address.

So none of this was new to us as a faculty. If we had not heard it before, and most of us had, we certainly knew it from personal experience. We also knew that the consultant was correct in his advice, and Ed and I hoped the team approach would finally begin to encourage teachers to implement strategies to meet those needs. WATERSHED, we knew, was one such strategy which already had a record of proven success. Now, at last, an outside authority was supporting our approach.

In fact, the consultant started singing our praises and extolling our virtues to every audience who would listen. He wanted to write articles and maybe even a book about WATERSHED; and he used WATERSHED as an example, at least in general terms, at many of the other schools with which he worked. Numerous school districts contacted us for further information based on this consultant's recommendations.

Unfortunately, despite his advice and his expertise on the middle level child, few of his suggestions translated into working reality. Furthermore, when several other teachers put forward ideas for whole learning programs similar to WATERSHED, though using different central themes, all were refused. The reasons given for their lack of acceptance made just enough sense to be plausible, but not enough sense to be valid. I felt like that Lenape sachem for whom the initial thrill of owning a metal hatchet finally paled with the realization of what he had ultimately lost in the bargain.

Since then, the other teams, for the most past, have simply maintained the same traditional format of segregated classes and conventional schedules they used before the advent of teaming. Some teams have dabbled in interdisciplinary mini-units and activities, and they are to be commended. However, some team teachers share little in common beyond the fact that the same student names appear on their respective class lists.

One other seventh grade team has tried to implement some changes. They now use some of WATERSHED's activities, and they even visit some of the same places we do. They do so, however, without the central, unifying concept; and they continue to employ a traditional class schedule of segregated disciplines in a conventional time format. As a result, substantive improvements from our point of view have been minimal.

Unfortunately, these limited improvements have been just enough to lull people into thinking that the basic problem has been resolved and the urgency for serious change removed. While some of the symptoms have been temporarily controlled, the underlying illness persists.

Outside visitation teams brought in during the spring of 1991 and again in 1992 saw the very limited existence of real teaming and commented on it in their respective reports. The first of these teams came to assess the teaching of science in our district. The second came specifically to evaluate the middle school's transition to teaming.

The science education evaluation report (1991) generally described the quality of science instruction within our district as adequate but suffering from certain deficiencies. The most notable exception to any criticism, however, was the WATERSHED program, which the report singled out as "an example of appropriate educational strategy for the 1990s." (p. 5) Asserting that "the WATERSHED program is an outstanding example of such a 'hands-on' program" (p. 50) and of "cooperative learning strategies and a de-emphasis on competition" (p. 54), the report went on to assert that "the WATERSHED program is an excellent example of how the delivery strategies are highly consistent with the findings and recommendations of professional science teaching organizations" (pp. 54-55). Then, after praising WATERSHED for its "abundant evidence of writing in journals on a regular basis" (p. 57), the report concluded that "the WATERSHED Program, again, stands as a superb example of everything that an interdisciplinary approach can be if appropriate variances from standard curricular practices are granted" (p. 65).

Though admittedly biased, I find the evaluation team's report remarkable. After all, in WATERSHED we never recognize any activity as solely one of *science,* per se. Students do not label any concept or activity as being strictly "scientific." We never claim, as do traditional curricula through their time block/subject area scheduling, "now we're doing biology," or "now we're learning chemistry." Students are not told, "Put away the history books; it's time for science." Instead, WATERSHED students experience all concepts and all activities in an integrated, whole learning fashion. Yet, despite this non-traditional approach, the independent panel of science educators clearly saw in WATERSHED something of value for science education. Obviously the students were learning about science and about scientific issues and methods without taking a science course, per se.

WATERSHED students experience all concepts and all activities in an integrated, whole learning fashion.

The second team of independent evaluators, looking more specifically at the issue of teaming in our middle schools, also recognized a special value to the WATERSHED program. In the report the team noted: "Radnor

Middle School does have some problems and concerns that need to be addressed. Most involve unresolved conflicts created by an incomplete transition to the middle level concept in certain areas. Traditional approaches to scheduling and time use will not suffice for a true middle school" (p. 6). The panel further asserted that "the transition to a middle level concept requires a new and creative approach to scheduling" (p. 14). In addition, the panel recognized WATERSHED as being perhaps "one of the most innovative programs in the nation" (p. 10), and they recommended that our staff and administration "explore the possibility of offering other innovative programs like the WATERSHED Project" (p. 11).

During a staff in-service program set up to examine the conclusions and recommendations of the 1992 visitation team, our own faculty concurred with the observations of the visitation team but did not expand the whole learning approach. To many, whole learning programs such as WATERSHED are viewed as trivial or something extra to be offered like an elective to some students. The whole learning approach, however, is a workable solution to many of the very problems teachers seek to resolve.

I am reminded of an incident that occurred on our end-of-the-year family canoe trip one June. After paddling for awhile in the hot sun, a number of us stopped to use a rope swing. One after another, students—and even some parents—climbed up the three foot bank, stepped up onto one of two twin cantilevered sycamore branches, grabbed a thick rope suspended from a higher branch, swung Tarzan-like out over the river, let go, and plunged playfully into the refreshing water. I stood in the stream below the branches to act as a safety spotter and to help pass the rope back to the next swinger. One girl, the younger sister of one of our WATER-SHED students, reached for the rope, slipped, and fell between the two branches. She caught hold of one branch just before her feet hit the water. Scraped and scared, she hung there crying. I reached up, grabbed her waist gently, and urge her to let go of the branch. Even as I assured her that she had but six more inches to drop safely into the water, and even as her parents and friends reassured her, she refused to let go. So great was her fear that she held to that branch, even as that action continued to cause her pain. When her strength finally lapsed, she slid safely and easily into the stream. Ten minutes later she was splashing, laughing, and rope-swinging again. Tangentially, two years later this same young lady became a WATERSHED participant, and we continue to laugh about that incident.

That student learned a lesson most of her teachers still have not learned. In the face of serious problems, we as teachers often refuse to let go of our old ways, even though a new and workable solution is within easy reach.

We cling to outmoded and unworkable methods even as students, parents, and outside visitation teams recognize and recommend ways to get safely back into the current.

Each year the success of the program becomes more evident. Visitors to WATERSHED, as well as parents, students, and independent evaluation teams continue to praise the program. Many bemoan the fact that WATER-SHED remains unique, and they urge the creation in Radnor of more whole learning programs as models. While I, too, am disappointed that more whole learning programs have not yet been implemented in Radnor, I am pleased to report that some neighboring school districts are currently in the process of adapting WATERSHED to their middle schools. As of this writing, I know of three such new programs that are slated to commence with the opening of schools this September

In addition to recognition by outside evaluators, WATERSHED gained from the middle school's transition to teaming a much better classroom location. Furthermore, unlike our Lenape predecessors, we had the opportunity to affect the shape of our new home.

WATERSHED took over a large open space area previously called "the Commons" located right by the bus entrance. This space was split in two, a small side and a much larger side by the placement of the outer doors and the walkway students used to pass from their busses to the classrooms. Two new interior walls, complete with beautiful display cases, created a small classroom and a large classroom as big as our old one, with the public entry way remaining in between them. To the larger side we added a small darkroom, two sinks, a walk-in storage closet, and a small coat closet. We also added an emergency exit door, blackboards, some cabinets, and a phone with an outside line. Our math teacher, Woody Arnold, who for the first three years of the program had been located two floors below us and seldom seen, moved into the smaller classroom across the newly created entrance foyer. Our team was now together—in more ways than one.

Encouraged by the exciting prospects of this physical change of space, Ed and I decided that the time had come to change the subject of our studies as well. Though we could easily have devoted many years to the study of the Brandywine, we wanted to see if our ideas could readily be transferred to other streams—in particular, other streams with perhaps fewer obvious advantages. We saw this as a crucial point. While every school district in the country is located in a watershed, not every watershed would contain a stream as overtly significant as the Brandywine with all its historical and cultural importance. If we wanted similar programs to spread to other school districts, we had to demonstrate that the approach could work equally well with smaller streams such as those any school district might encompass within its boundaries.

Once again, keep in mind that I am advocating in this book the proliferation of the whole learning philosophy, not merely the spread of stream or watershed studies. Yet, I also recognize the conservative nature of most educators. When faced with a novel idea or approach such as the whole learning method I am advocating, many educators will look for the path of least resistance should they elect to try that new approach. In this case, that would mean trying to implement a proven program before trying to develop an entirely new one of their own. So, while I recognize and encourage the potential use of numerous different central themes, I also see the need to show that this program in particular, with its watershed/stream study theme, could be transferred to smaller streams in other areas as a way to introduce the whole learning philosophy and methodology to other school systems.

To this end, then, we decided to switch streams. While finding new streams would certainly not be a problem, working with some of them created a major environmental dilemma. Even on the Brandywine, an eighth order stream, we experienced occasional difficulties minimizing the physical impact of forty seventh graders visiting specific locations. On a tiny second, third, or fourth order stream, that impact could prove truly devastating. Clearly a new approach would be required, at least in terms of our field study procedures.

Up to this point, we had always taken the entire class together on field study trips to the Brandywine. On those trips we divided the students into five groups. The groups changed with each trip to ensure that every student would work with all the others during the year. Each group had a water testing kit, a thermometer, meter sticks, a tennis ball, and rope which they carried in an inexpensive plastic crate such as the ones in which milk bottles used to be delivered. Each group was assigned a section of the stream, usually about thirty meters or so from the next group.

At their site, the students first drew sketches of the area and wrote descriptions or sometimes poetry. Then the students worked together to measure the width of the stream using the ropes and meter sticks. At the same time, they took depth measurements every meter. Once they had determined the width, the students divided that width by five. This gave them the locations at which they had to measure the velocity of the stream. For example, if the stream were twenty-five meters wide at their site, the students would divide twenty-five by five, which of course yielded an answer of five meters. The students would then take velocity readings at four points located every five meter across the stream. This they accomplished by timing how long it took a tennis ball to float one meter at each of the four predetermined points. From this physical data, the students found an average depth and an average velocity. Then they determined the volume, or flow, of the stream by multiplying the average depth times the average velocity times the width times a bottom constant which accounted for the friction along the stream bed. This constant would be a .8 for a rocky stream bed, a .9 for a sandy or smooth stream bed. Students recorded all this data, along with temperature readings and descriptions of the weather.

At their site, students first drew sketches of the area

...and wrote descriptions or sometimes poetry.

Once the physical characteristics of the stream had been determined, the students moved on to the chemical parameters. Using relatively simple and inexpensive tests purchased from the HACH company, the students tested the stream water for dissolved oxygen, dissolved carbon dioxide, nitrates, phosphates, and pH. From each of these readings the group had to draw conclusions about the health of the stream.

To augment their chemical conclusions, the students also searched for benthic invertebrates. At first we used simple rock testing methods whereby students merely pick up fist-sized rocks from the stream bed and see what is crawling on it. Later we tried kick screens, and eventually we moved on to more sophisticated serber sampling techniques. Regardless of the collected method employed, the students learned to identify the various organisms which inhabit the streams, to understand the degree to which each was pollution tolerant, and to draw conclusions about the quality of the stream based on this information.

Back in the classroom, all this physical, chemical, and biotic data was logged, charted, and graphed. The results from each of the five groups were compared first to determine significant differences, if any, at the site. Then we looked at results from the same site at earlier times to look for changes, and finally we compared the site to other sites in the region.

We knew the problem did not lie with the general testing procedure. We would continue to take all the same measurements, but we just could not continue to do it with forty students at one time on tiny streams. Using our Brandywine Saga summer program experiences as a guide, we knew the solution lay in abandoning the large group approach to field testing. Instead of taking forty students to various locations, Ed or I could take ten in a van. The rest of the class would remain with the other one of us and continue to work on projects.

The advantages of this new approach became immediately apparent. Above and beyond the environmental benefits, this method would allow us greater contact with each of the testing groups, and the ability to work more closely with individual students both in the field and back in the classroom. Furthermore, van trips cost far less than bus trips; in fact, each van day represented less than a quarter of the expenses involved in using a bus for a day. By taking two van groups per day, we cut our transportation expenses in half. Finally, using vans and taking smaller groups of students meant we could visit and test more sites, even on smaller streams, that were inaccessible to a bus.

To be honest, there is also a downside to this procedure: the loss of an important shared group experience. To make up for this, we have continued to take the whole group on some field test outings, usually involving a site to which we can walk. We also involve the entire class in the recording and the analysis of data gathered by the smaller testing groups. Overall, I believe the advantages of the newer approach far outweigh the disadvantages.

Thus, for year number four we left the Brandywine and decided to study the six smaller streams which drain our own Delaware County. We divided the class into six groups, each responsible for examining one of the six streams and sharing their results with the class. Year Four was an unusual year in many ways, and I will discuss that at greater length in the next chapter. However, for the moment it needs be admitted that our plans proved overly ambitious. Six streams turned out to be too many, at least four too many. We learned a lot, to be sure, and our general procedures continued to work admirably on the smaller waterways thus demonstrating that the program could be transferred readily to other streams. The group, however, suffered in other important ways. We were spread too thinly. So, at the risk of getting ahead of the story, for year number five we opted to compare just two local streams, Gulph and Darby creeks, which drain most of Radnor Township.

Nevertheless, planning for the diversity of studying six streams simultaneously in year four prompted us to find a new organizing principle. We needed a thread or a group of threads that would tie all six stream studies together and bind them as a cohesive whole. We thought of several different topic ideas and strategies, but they all seemed to divide rather than unify the year. Finally we hit upon three general emphases that not only tied the six stream studies together, but which fit together beautifully. Instead of the original research report approach we had been using, we decided to examine the streams through the senses of *Place, Time,* and *Quality.*

The *Sense of Place,* with which we now open the WATERSHED year, establishes the physical parameters of whatever stream or streams we decide to study. This accounts for concepts of geography and geomorphology, and for concepts of natural cycles, processes, plants, and animals as well. It also directly relates the specific physical, chemical, and biotic aspects of our field testing procedures to these larger regional factors.

Within *Sense of Place* we incorporated many of the projects and reports formerly used. For example, the plant and animal reports remained, as did many of the special essays such as the "Drip" essay and the "Insects of the Water's Surface" essay. In the first of these, the student becomes a drop of water who experiences the water cycle and a journey along one of our study streams. Along that journey, the drop reviews important places and encounters plants and animals that live in the creek. In the second story, the student becomes a waterstrider, a springtail, a backswimmer, or a whirligig beetle and describes a day in his or her life on the surface of the stream. In both cases, the students must pull together and use the information they have learned and their specific knowledge of a particular stream's location and ecology.

The students continue to spend a great deal of time working with maps in the *Sense of Place*. They locate their own homes on a map of the township and identify the particular watershed in which they live. They study regional maps to discern how the streams we are studying fit into larger watersheds. And, of course, they continue to construct their own three dimensional topographical map of the watershed in question.

All of these activities in the classroom work hand-in-hand with the numerous autumn field testing and geology trips to help the students develop a Sense of Place, an understanding of where they are and of what the region is like physically.

The middle portion of our year, which we call *Sense of Time,* allows us to view our streams in a chronological fashion. This includes continuing to look at the geological and geomorphological factors as they have changed over time. It further allows us to begin the examination of the interrelationships that exist between the watersheds and the peoples who have inhabited them. The Lenni-Lenape, the early Swedish colonists, the Quakers to whom I have referred throughout this book, along with the myriad other immigrants who came to Pennsylvania all played crucial roles in shaping the land and the streams as we know them today. These people, in turn, have been indelibly shaped and altered by the region as well. Thus, to understand the region and, what is more, to understand ourselves, we have to have a *Sense of Time.*

At various points in this portion of the year the students write "American Diaries" wherein they imagine themselves a Pre-Columbian Lenape, a Swedish colonist, a Quaker miller's apprentice, or a participant in the Battle of the Brandywine, and they describe a day in their life at that time. The students also create a colony, using their knowledge from *Sense of Place.* They research a few years of the nineteenth century and create a newspaper to share their research with the class. They conduct debates, construct hanging timelines of important events, and describe the cultures of major immigrant groups, their ancestors, who represent the population of our region.

Ultimately this brings us up to the present and to a *Sense of Quality*. What are the watersheds of our region like today? How are the various systems within a watershed similar to the systems which comprise our house and even our own bodies. How do our actions effect all aspects of life within the watershed? What might these local watersheds be like in the near future? Will we continue to espouse the old European land ethic; that is, continue to see ourselves as separate from the watersheds we inhabit? Or, will we perhaps begin to understand and accept a world view wherein all things are interrelated, much as the Lenape believed? Clearly, WATER-SHED through its content and its whole learning structure promotes this latter concept—for watersheds and for education.

So, we moved on to a new room, new streams, and a new structure. Yet we retained and, I believe, refined the relationships between the philosophy and the implementation of whole learning.

Again, I think the Lenape spirits would be pleased. ₩

United We Stand; Divided . . .

Dan Hoffman
'94

Beyond the city limits, to the west of Philadelphia's older suburbs, lies the area through which flow the Brandywine River and the other streams we study. Delaware and Chester counties, once a unified part of William Penn's original land grant, remain famous to this day for their pastoral tranquility. Built over two hundred years ago, solid stone farmhouses and bank barns still dot the gently rolling Piedmont landscape, real models for many of Andrew Wyeth's famous paintings. The local streams on their steady descent toward the fall line and the coastal plain beyond meander playfully among fields and forests, hedges, and highways.

For all its tranquility, however, and despite its heritage of both Lenape and Quaker non-violence, this region has witnessed more than its share of conflict. Most recently, environmentalists and concerned citizens have battled utility companies and land developers in an on-going, all-out legal war of deeds, easements and right-of-ways, suits and countersuits. The land around Andrew Wyeth's home along the Brandywine, for example, continues to bear the scars wrought by a gas company victorious in its fight to secure a right-of-way for its pipeline through the very heart of the valley. On the other side of the battle, concerned citizens won a victory when they managed to save an old grist mill from being razed. By so doing, they thwarted plans to erect oil storage tanks on that site along the Brandywine and instead converted that old grist mill into the world famous Brandywine River Museum.

Victories such as that don't happen often enough, however, even with the on-going, vigilant efforts of the Brandywine Conservancy. On every field study trip we lament the loss of yet another tree or the arrival of yet another house somewhere in the region. Mini-malls and condominium complexes spread through the fields like poison ivy, while the local newspapers give us daily reports from the front in the form of articles on planning board meetings and ads for real estate sales.

Too little of the valley of the Brandywine countryside remains pastoral.

Yet, of all the battles waged over these watersheds, perhaps the most famous were those fought here a little over two hundred years ago during America's War for Independence. The Brandywine River and the Wissahickon Creek near Germantown, at opposite ends of our study area, witnessed during September and October of 1777 the two bloodiest battles of that revolution. The respective actions that autumn of George Washington and his British counterpart, General Howe, led directly to the Continental Army's bitter yet glorious winter encampment at Valley Forge, which also lies within our study area.

Besides being the second bloodiest battle of the war, the Battle of the Brandywine, fought on September 11, 1777, stands as one of that war's most enigmatic conflicts as well. Events that day illustrated the tenuous nature of the revolution in the eyes of the local populace and demonstrated the tenacious character of the inexperienced Continental Army. The day showed Anthony Wayne and the young Marquis de Lafayette at their best, but left unanswered doubts about Washington's competence and Howe's resolve. What is more, the outcome of the battle related directly to the river and its surrounding topography—precisely the sort of interrelationship we want WATERSHED students to examine.

To make a long story short, in the summer of 1777, General Howe decided that if he could capture the colonial capital of Philadelphia, the fledgling Continental Army would lose its will and disband. The war would end quickly, and thousands of lives would be spared. Even if worse came to worst, and the war dragged on, at least Howe and his army would have comfortable quarters in cosmopolitan Philadelphia for the coming winter. So, Howe loaded all his men and supplies onto ships and set sail.

Washington, suspecting Howe wanted Philadelphia, circulated rumors that the Delaware River was heavily fortified and blocked by sunken vessels. Whether this was true or not, Howe decided not to try that approach and headed instead for the Chesapeake Bay. A severe storm wracked Howe's fleet during August, and neither his men nor his horses fared well. When he finally landed his army near Elkton, Maryland in the closing days of August, his men were sick, tired, virtually horseless, and no closer to Philadelphia that they had been when in New York. Howe rested his troops for several days and scoured the countryside commandeering horses for his cavalry, his artillery, and his baggage wagons.

Washington, in the meantime, pulled his forces out of New Jersey and Philadelphia and headed southwest toward Chester and Wilmington. He knew that the Brandywine River would be his best line of natural defense between the British and Philadelphia. It also offered a buffer shielding the

Great Valley, then America's breadbasket, from the on-coming British. So, Washington watched Howe's movements carefully and tried to figure out where Sir William would finally attempt his crossing.

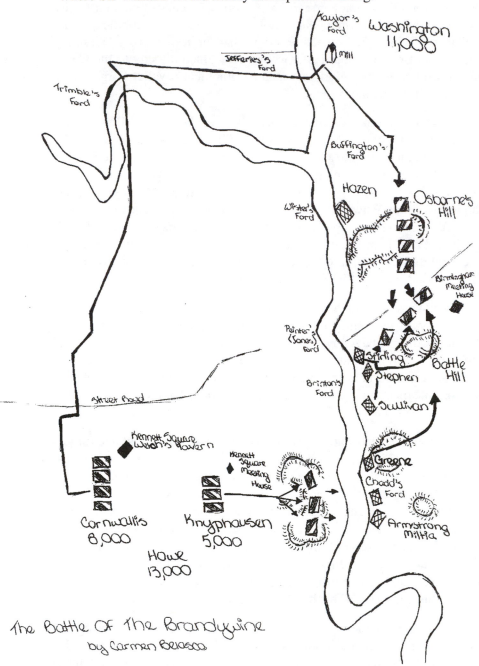

The Battle Of The Brandywine
by Carmen Belasca

To anyone traveling the region today, it is easy to believe that Washington must have smiled smugly when he learned that the British were marching up the King's Highway, now Route 1, toward Chaddsford on the Brandywine. The topography there is a defending general's dream, an attacking general's worst nightmare. Directly south of Chaddsford for several miles steep, muddy banks line the river separating its course from high, rugged, forested hills. This area marks the beginning of the narrow canyon formed by the river as it crosses the fall line, plummeting 125 feet in its final four miles to Wilmington and the coastal plain. No army would attempt that southern route.

At Chaddsford itself, the river's flood plain broadens out to over half a mile in width. It is open and marshy. More importantly, gently rolling ridges to both the east and the west command controlling views of this wide floodplain, with the eastern hills being the higher of the two. It was here that Washington must have smiled as he positioned his artillery.

Only four miles to the northwest, the river forks into its east and west branches, the site of our first river sharing circle two hundred and ten years later, almost to the day. Between Chaddsford and the forks lie four additional fords, and Washington sent troops to guard all of them. On the surface, this seems a wise military decision; but, in reality, it points out the puzzle historians have yet to explain adequately.

Further to the north and west the two branches wind their respective ways slowly through the south ridge and into the Great Valley. Beyond that, they meander through the tree-covered north ridge to their seeps in the Welsh Hills. All this way, the branches narrow to average widths of less than twenty meters, and shallow to average depths of less than half a meter. Given this fact, and the relatively short marching distances involved, one wonders why Washington did not seem to concern himself with crossings further upstream. As an experienced surveyor, he had to be aware of the topographical implications of the area, even if he was not personally familiar with the specifics of the region. As an experienced commander, he should have foreseen the possibility of a flanking maneuver, particularly since he had suffered an embarrassing defeat on Long Island when the same enemy general had managed to encircle him. Perhaps he felt the distances were sufficiently great to allow him reaction time should he learn of such a flanking movement. Yet, Washington knew he could not rely on the local populace for intelligence regarding British troop movements. The pacifistic Quakers steadfastly refused to have anything to do with the conflict. Nevertheless, Washington seemed satisfied with posting pickets only as far as Buffington's Ford at the forks of the Brandywine.

Warm days followed by cool nights frequently bring damp fogs to the valley in September. Accounts suggest that this was the case that Thursday morning, September 11, 1777, as two thousand Hessian artillerymen marched out of Kennett Square and took position on the high ground to the west of the Brandywine near Chaddsford. Meanwhile, Generals Howe and Cornwallis marched a much larger force northeastward. They crossed the west branch of the Brandywine at Trimble's Ford, about a mile above the forks. Then they similarly crossed the east branch at Jefferies's Ford. The Colonial pickets at Buffington's Ford near the forks apparently never saw or heard the main British army pass within a half mile of them.

By the time Washington learned of Howe's advance, it was too late. The trap had been sprung. Leaving Anthony Wayne to hold Chaddsford and guard the rear to prevent a pincer movement, Washington pulled the rest of his troops from their defensive positions along the Brandywine. These troops had to run, quite literally, up a mile of steep hillside to engage the British who now held the higher ground near Birmingham Friends Meetinghouse.

The ensuing action cost Washington dearly. Despite the valiant efforts of many, including those of young Lafayette who was wounded in the battle, Washington was forced to withdraw from the field at dusk. Under the cover of darkness, with Anthony Wayne guarding his retreat, Washington fled with the remnants of his army eastward to Chester.

Howe, rather than pursuing the defeated Continentals, chose to let his army rest in Chaddsford for several days. Then, as Washington pulled back into Philadelphia, Howe marched north a few short miles into the Great Valley looking for food.

When they heard about the defeat at Brandywine, and fearing capture in Philadelphia, the Continental Congress fled to Lancaster, Pennsylvania. This left Washington with a new problem: Howe's movement toward the Great Valley put him in a position to come between Washington's army and the Congress. So, Washington headed westward again to protect the Congress. Along the way, he again engaged the British atop the south ridge of the Great Valley west of Malvern. Fortunately, at least for the Continentals, heavy, low storm clouds rolled in and the battle was rained out before any further damage was inflicted. Had it not been for that fortuitous interplay of weather and topography, the revolution might well have ended right there near the headwaters of Ridley Creek. As it was, however, Washington passed the British and moved westward to shield the Congress. Once again he left Anthony Wayne behind to keep tabs on and harass the British.

Just four nights later, on September 20, Howe dispatched Hessian troops under the cover of night to bayonet Wayne's troops as the slept along the headwaters of Crum Creek. The infamous Paoli Massacre forced Wayne to retreat, and Howe moved freely across the Schuylkill River, ironically at Valley Forge, to set up camp just outside of Philadelphia in Germantown.

Here Washington saw his chance to avenge his recent series of humiliating defeats. He put together a brilliant attack plan which seemed to guarantee success. The best made plans, however, often go astray. Once again weather and topography played havoc with Washington's strategy. Compounding the problem, one of Washington's generals was drunk, arrived late to the battle and, in the fog and smoke of that early October morning, ended up firing on Anthony Wayne's men who had made more progress than expected. Another general, who was supposed to have entered the field from the flank, feared a counter-attack and refused to advance on schedule across the ravine of the Wissahickon Creek to entrap Howe's retreating troops. The results again proved disastrous: the Continental ranks were depleted, and the Battle of Germantown earned the dubious distinction of being the bloodiest battle of the American Revolution.

Howe's army subsequently spent a delightful winter in Philadelphia. The tattered remnants of Washington's army dragged themselves back across the Schuylkill River to the relative safety of the heights around Valley Forge. There, through the winter of 1777 and 1778, they licked their wounds, froze, starved, and trained themselves into a discipline fighting force.

Students visit Valley Forge in the winter.

In a great many ways, the fourth year of WATERSHED paralleled the events of that turbulent and painful period.

Like Washington, Ed and I should have been better prepared. We certainly had ample warning signs. When our class list for Year Four came out in the late spring of Year Three, several fifth and sixth grade teachers shook their head in disbelief. One laughed derisively, and one intimated that the computer must have been out to get us.

Ed and I prefer not to listen to doomsayers. We have certainly experienced our share of them, and we have found that they are generally wrong—particularly since many of the pessimists base their judgments on students' behavior in traditional classroom settings which too frequently encourage discipline problems through boring, irrelevant teaching strategies and lockstep rigidity. We generally have far fewer discipline problems in WATERSHED because the students tend to enjoy the work, they see a purpose for that work, and they respond positively to the freedom and responsibility granted to them. Many students who have had discipline problems in earlier grades proved to be delightful youngsters who just did not fit the traditional system. Once freed from those artificial constraints, many blossomed both behaviorally and academically. We had certainly witnessed this, as described earlier, in Year Three.

Beyond this factor, the fact that we have our students for virtually the whole day, every day, allows us to take a different approach to the whole matter of discipline. First, we get the chance to deal with problems in long range terms. We are not compelled by conventional time limits to over-react or to deal harshly and sharply with situations. We can work with the student, not against the student, toward a gradual but sincere modification of his or her behavior.

When a teacher has to deal each day with over a hundred students in groups, which meet for only forty-five minutes or so, and that teacher is responsible for covering a prescribed amount of a curriculum besides, there is very little opportunity for that teacher to provide individualized attention. It does not matter how great the teacher may be, the time simply does not exist. Many behavioral problems result directly from this time pressure and from the lack of personalized attention it causes. Take, for example, the all too common case of students who act up out of frustration because they just do not understand a concept. The teacher has neither the time to recognize this gap adequately (until it shows up on a test—causing even more frustration for the child) or to redress it. Then, to make matters even worse, when the child acts out his frustration, he or she is generally rewarded not with help but with punishment. The child is caught in a no-win, catch-22 dilemma. So, too, is the teacher.

In WATERSHED, the time we share allows us to understand the students' problems more fully, simply because we get the chance to know them better. We have the time and the physical continuity to develop significant rapport and mutual trust with our students. Teachers and students are partners and co-learners in the process of education. We have the time to give each student more individualized attention.

We also have the time to employ more flexible classroom management strategies which promote rather than restrict student freedom and the responsible use of that freedom. The students make frequent choices as to how to use their time, and for much of any given day they have the freedom to move about the room. Together, all these factors greatly reduce student frustration and the stress that comes with the inability to move for extended periods, and to increase the students' sense of having a positive vested interest in the educational process. By so doing, the whole learning approach reduces the adversarial nature of the all too typical student-teacher relationship which, in turn, makes discipline far less of an issue.

The whole learning approach reduces the adversarial nature of the typical student-teacher relationship.

We also get the time to work more closely with the parents than do most teachers. The whole learning system of weekly communication and efforts to encourage active parental participation ensure more cooperative involvement by all parties in the search for the most effective ways to help each student. Put all this together, and discipline tends to be far less of a problem for us than for some traditional classroom teachers.

As a result, we try not to give too much significance to other teachers' predictions or prophesies of impending doom. And thus we entered Year Four with the same naive self-assurance that Washington must have felt as he aligned his troops along the eastern banks of the Brandywine.

In all honesty and fairness, most of the students that year were, as individuals, as delightful as any other students I have ever had. Some still rank among my personal favorites, and I look forward to a lifetime of following their growth and accomplishments. As a group, however, the chemistry was altogether different. At least eight came to us with severe emotional problems. Two or three of these were downright anti-social and openly malicious in all of their actions toward others.

As a result, the group rarely functioned together well at all. The positive efforts of many individual students encountered open condemnation by the all too vocal minority of troubled students. We tried numerous

alternative groupings and different kinds of projects. We tried with varying degrees of success to work with the parents. We even brought in the
guidance counselor, who tried to conduct lessons in conflict resolution
and cooperation. All to no avail. In fact, some of the most troubled and
troublesome students refused to see that their negative behavior was a
problem. To some of them, hurtful actions were apparently the norm, to
some even enjoyable.

Since they felt and acted as they did, when asked why they had even
opted to be in WATERSHED, several candidly admitted that they had chosen to participate in WATERSHED so someone else who truly wanted to
be in the program would not get the chance. Obviously that attitude does
not go far toward promoting cooperation, commitment, or caring.

I must admit that we inadvertently compounded the problem. As I
explained previously in Chapter Six, we shifted our study focus for Year
Four from the Brandywine to the six smaller streams that drain our county.
To accommodate this change, we randomly divided the class into six groups,
each of which was responsible for the study of one of the streams. At the
time, this made sense environmentally and educationally; much as I am
sure Washington's decision to guard only four fords made sense to him at
the time. In retrospect, however, this was clearly a mistake which served
to further de-emphasize the very unity we needed so desperately to foster.

Despite all the problems, good things somehow did occur that year.
Among other positive accomplishments, a dozen or so students worked
together with me and a high school student to write, film, and edit two
wonderful videos about out water testing procedures. Some of our most
creative individual projects and art work were also completed that year.

Still, my most vivid recollections of the year unfortunately concern
the conflicts, both verbal and physical, among students. Ed and I both
came close to calling it quits. I contemplated a change of careers. We kept
ourselves going in the final months of that year, I am ashamed to admit, by
falling back into a more typical teacher mode. In a sense, we conceded our
losses and directed most of our efforts toward those positive students whose
WATERSHED experience also was being marred by the personal problems of those few. We found it also helped us to keep in mind that we each
had sufficient sick days accumulated to take the remainder of the year off
if conditions grew totally unbearable. (Just for the record, neither of us
missed a single day.)

That year's final sharing circle in June was a different affair. I faced it
with sincere trepidation. I must admit that I felt truly relieved that the year

was over, a feeling I had never felt before in my teaching career, and one which I hope never to feel again. Yet, to my surprise, we again witnessed the tears and the reluctance to leave which we see every year. Somehow, all the trials and tribulations and all the bad times had brought the majority of this group together in the end. Somehow, like the soldiers who suffered at Valley Forge, many of these students used the hardships to their advantage and came out the stronger for it. Some of those with the severest problems continued to suffer through eighth grade; some continue to suffer today. Yet reports from the eighth grade teachers the following year were tremendously positive, to the point where I began to doubt my sanity—or at the very least my memory. Even some of the fifth and sixth grade teachers noted the change and asked what we had done to cause them. In all honesty, I don't know that we did anything, except perhaps allow them the time and the opportunity to work through their problems in a less threatening or foreboding milieu. At any rate, now in high school, many of these same youngsters are doing quite well academically and socially.

Are there risks in trying to implement a whole learning program like WATERSHED. Year Four showed us quite clearly that there are indeed dangers. One of my closest friends and teaching associates, whom I tried to convince to start a second whole learning program like WATERSHED, declined because he did not want to take the risk of having to be with the same students for such an extended period of time. He knew it could prove wonderfully exhilarating, as it has for Ed and me most years; but he feared the alternative possibility of being trapped in a horrible situation with a negative group.

Looking back on it all, I cannot help but attribute part of the problem we experienced in Year Four, and part of the potential danger which prevented my friend from trying the whole learning type of approach, to the fact that the students continue to lack a true choice. Being the only game in town, WATERSHED attracted some students merely because it is not regular school. Had these students had more alternative, whole learning programs from which to choose, perhaps their truer interests might have been more readily engaged. This, in turn, might have enabled some of them to have a better experience. Perhaps, then, the more of us willing to take the risk, the lower the risk becomes. From my point of view, it is certainly worth a try.

After all, every revolution involves risks. Every struggle has its losses and setbacks. The value comes from confronting the risks. Mistakes can be made, battles can be lost, but victory ultimately comes when the dangers are overcome and the risks are turned into assets. **ᗯ**

Manifest Destinies?   8.

Since the end of the Revolutionary War, this part of southeastern Pennsylvania has reflected all the major trends and changes that have characterized the growth and development of the United States through that same period. As the new nation formed and reformed itself, colonial enterprises gave way to rapid industrial growth throughout the nineteenth century. In this area, for example, the DuPont family settled along the banks of the Brandywine during the first years of the nineteenth century and began manufacturing their high quality black powder. Nationally, America's population increased rapidly during the nineteenth century. Locally, the population swelled as wave after wave of immigrants found their way to Philadelphia. Some of these merely passed through on their way west. Many stayed to fill the growing need for industrial laborers and to add new and colorful patches to the crazy-quilt of our local culture.

In the eighteenth century, Charles Mason and Jeremiah Dixon had seen fit to create their famous dividing line right through this area. In fact, the very spot from which they took their astronomical observations to survey that line is to this day marked by their "Star Gazers' Stone," a small monument just several hundred meters from the Brandywine River in Embreeville, Pennsylvania. That line, as we all know, became the symbolic boundary between slave and free states in the years preceding the Civil War.

While this area witnessed no great battles of that war, nor even minor skirmishes to my knowledge, it nevertheless played a critical role in that conflict. A major spur of the Underground Railroad ran right through this region, and countless slaves found their way to freedom by traveling secretly from one Quaker farmhouse to another.

Even before the start of that figurative railroad, one of America's first iron tracks transected the streams we study. This line, dubbed the Columbia Railroad, ran from Philadelphia to Columbia, Maryland. It became the seed that would eventually blossom into the main line of one of America's legendary railroad companies, the Pennsylvania Railroad. In fact, the region in which Radnor is situated is to this day referred to as "the Mainline," and the town of Wayne, then called Louella, was one of the early suburbs to spring up along the tracks. It is no coincidence that those tracks parallel an old Lenape trail which became the Lincoln Highway, otherwise known as U.S. Route 30. Nor is it a coincidence that the trail turned highway follows the ridge lines separating the Gulph and Darby creek watersheds as it passes through our study area.

The stresses and strains of national expansion and industrialization clearly affected this region. A counter argument can be made that the region affected these trends as well. Natural resources, including soil and mineral wealth, the power of our streams falling from the Piedmont to the coastal plain, the deep water ports on the Delaware, all of these features of the land attracted people and provided the means for the very growth and development that would in turn alter our region and make it what it is today.

In much the same way, the trials of Year Four, along with the successes of the three previous years, caused us to change WATERSHED somewhat in the ensuing years. For one thing, we decided that the purely random selection process might not be the best way to determine the participants, at least not as long as WATERSHED was the sole alternative to the traditional program. Even with the problems of Year Four, WATERSHED had become a very popular option. The vast majority of students openly asserted their wish to be in WATERSHED, or at least out of the conventional curriculum. A similarly large number of parents likewise lobbied to get their children into WATERSHED. Yet, as was noted earlier, some students selected at random by the computer elected to join the program for the wrong reasons. These students did not get as much as they might have out of the experience, and they eliminated others who had a sincere desire to participate. This had directly impacted on the quality of Year Four, as we have seen, and we did not want to see that happen again.

The problem was to reduce the likelihood of students participating merely because their name happened to be drawn by a computer, while still allowing every interested student an equal chance of being selected.

As we looked toward the selection of the next group, we decided to try yet another approach. What if students had to apply? Several arguments came immediately to mind. First, would this be fair? Did an application procedure by definition preclude certain students? Second, what would the application process entail? Again, would it be fair? We felt that the idea of applying was in itself a sign of sincere interest and was justified on that basis. When it was suggested that every student be given an application, we objected. That, we felt, took away from the students the very act of self-initiative and responsibility we wanted to see them evince.

After much discussion, we decided to make applications available to all students in several well-publicized locations, but the students had to come to those locations and request an application. This would allow them to demonstrate the motivation we wanted to see. Any student who then completed and turned in an application by a specified date would then be placed on the list for the computer. As before, the computer would create the final list of participants and alternates through a program of random selection, with bias only to ensure an equal number of boys and girls.

The application, itself, would include an overview of the program and a statement of expectations. These were to be read and signed by the student as well as his or her parents. In addition, the student was to write two brief essays. Once again, we worried that this might preclude some of our less academically oriented students. So, we agreed and made known that the essays would not be read until after the computer made its selections. Then they were read only as a way to help us get to know the incoming students. The act of completing the application, however, not the quality of the responses, made the student eligible for the computer list. A copy of that first application packet is included as Appendix E.

That spring 104 applications were turned in on time, and I later learned that a significant number came in after the deadline. These latter submissions were not included on the computer list, however, since the list was created and the randomizing program run at the close of school on the deadline date. Nevertheless, the applicant pool sent to the computer represented roughly 70% of the entire sixth grade class. Clearly the application procedure did not prevent interested students from demonstrating their desire to participate.

For Year Six we streamlined the process a bit further. We removed the essays from the original application. Our principal evidently received several complaints from parents whose children were not selected. These parents protested that it was unfair to make the students put time and effort into writing essays if those essays did not determine the selection. This seemed a valid point for sixth graders, so we made the essays a second step for those students who were selected by the computer. In other words, to be eligible for Year Six students had only to state their wish to be in the program by picking up a shortened form from specified locations, signing it, and returning it to the office by the prescribed deadline. If and when students were in fact selected, they confirmed their commitment by writing the two informational essays.

The response was once again overwhelming, amounting again to more than two thirds of the sixth grade population. Yet, despite the large number of applicants, for the most part this new procedure seemed to have removed from the eligibility pool most of the students who really had no interest in WATERSHED's unique approach and requirements. Those students simply chose not to apply.

Interestingly, it was the faculty of the large seventh grade team who most objected to the application procedure. They argued, not without some truth, that their student populations were randomly selected without choice or interest as factors, and so should be ours. At first glance, this appears to be a reasonable position. However, closer scrutiny reveals some flaws in the argument.

First, in all honesty, their groupings are not entirely random. Guidance counselors routinely make placement judgments. In fact, teachers are always polled to determine which students should not be put together on the same team, for example. In WATERSHED, we take which ever students the computer gives us; no engineering of the group is permitted. Second, within the larger team, itself, there is room to separate students if the need arises. No such option exists in WATERSHED.

In addition, the conventional nature of the traditional classes, and the fact that those teachers see a given group for only forty-five minutes or so at a time—and then only within the relatively safe confines of their classrooms—make the need for expressed interest less applicable. Students in the regular program are not as a general rule going to be expected to cooperate under the cold and wet, sometimes unpleasant and always potentially dangerous conditions WATERSHED students frequently confront on trips to streams. Nor will students in traditional teams be expected to "live" with each other in one room for six and a half hours each day, every day for the entire 184 days of our school year. Finally, the very nature of the WATERSHED experience as an alternative program demands, by definition, that the students want to be there.

Ideally, when whole learning becomes the norm and more programs like WATERSHED exist, every child will be able to select and be part of a program he or she truly wants to be in. Until that day, however, as long as programs such as WATERSHED are alternative programs, participation must be voluntary, based on real student interest.

We never did convince our colleagues on the 7A team; perhaps because during our fifth year they happened to have a group with negative chemistry, and WATERSHED's application process became their easy scapegoat. It is interesting to note that in Year Six their objections to the process disappeared. They had a "good" group that year, as did we. Besides, their class sizes went down again once 7B took on a third teacher and more students.

Year Five saw other changes directly attributable to our reactions to the problems of the fourth year. The frequent inability of the previous group to work harmoniously in small groups caused us to resurrect and implement a strategy of learning stations. This had been one of our original ideas, but it required too much planning and materials preparation time to be implemented feasibly in that first year of WATERSHED. We subsequently lost track of the notion as we developed and implemented the sequenced research project format described previously. As Year Four drew to a close and we found ourselves working more closely with individuals than with groups, we began to reconsider the idea of greater individualization of instruction. This would give even more responsibility to each student—not necessarily a bad thing in and of itself—and it would also enable students to progress even if others did not or could not. So, we set about structuring learning stations for each of the three phases of our WATERSHED year. As we began, we noted that two areas of our former work, microscopy and photography, were more method than content oriented. In short, they were tools which could be utilized in all three phases. So, we decided to set them up as permanent, year-long stations.

For our *Sense of Place* phase we established stations based on cartography, geology, ecology, and processes. Each station, in a designated area of the room, contained a box of index cards. Green index cards in each box described required tasks, while blue cards detailed recommended but optional activities. The required tasks tended, of course, to be the larger, most important tasks which called upon the students to use interrelationships among concepts to draw conclusions. The blue card activities were designed to help the students learn about smaller, or more specific concepts they would need in order to complete the required tasks successfully. These activities were also designed for enrichment and fun. In addition to the card boxes, each station housed the resources pertaining to the tasks involved.

At the cartography station, for example, the students learned about different types of maps from geopolitical to topographical. They learned to use a compass, to figure scale distances, and to interpret various maps. It was at this station that each child was required to make his or her own three dimensional topographic map of the watershed. Here, too, the students studied the climate and the weather of our region.

At the geology station the students learned about and mapped the locations of the rock formations which undergird our region. The students studied the geologic time scale to see how our region had changed over the millennia. They studied the rock cycle, and they drew conclusions about the ways rock formations determine topography.

For the ecology station the students researched the plants and animals of our area, much as students had done in all the previous years. The students also learned about food chains, food webs, and energy pyramids at this station.

At the processes station, the students discovered the intricacies of photosynthesis and respiration. They diagramed these processes, along with the nitrogen cycle and the hydrologic cycle as well.

Taken together, these learning stations provided the students with varied activities intended to help them understand the basic concept of a watershed. The stations directed their explorations into the reasons why watersheds are important, where our particular watershed is located, and how the watersheds we study are both similar and different.

The *Sense of Time* learning stations followed the chronology of the inhabitants: the Lenape, the Swedes, the Quakers, and the Revolutionary War. Each station included work with maps, the creation of an artifact, and an American Diary. The overall goal of these particular stations was to provide the students with a background knowledge of the various people who have lived in this area at different times, what their lives were like, and how they interacted with the streams.

By February, as we began to look at the nineteenth century, the nature of the work and the need for a more general survey seemed to us less suitable to the learning station format. So we returned to the newspaper project we had employed so successfully in previous years. Each student was assigned three or four years from the period between 1781 and 1915 or so. The students had to research these years and then put together a newspaper of major world and American events. The paper had to include maps, drawings, an editorial, and a feature section in addition to the specified number of news articles. When finished, each student presented his or her paper to the class in chronological order. This has always been a popular project with many of the students, and it allows us to cover and interrelate the major trends and developments of the nineteenth century rather rapidly.

For the *Sense of Quality* the students had just three learning stations, over and above the ongoing microscopy and photography tasks. The emphasis at each of these stations was on the systems that determine the quality of life. At one station the students had to study the systems of the human body and construct a "map" of those systems. They worked in pairs to make life-sized tracings of each other. Then they had to draw the organs and systems, cut them out of poster board, and place them properly within their traced bodies.

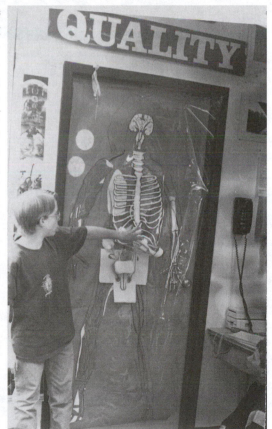

...students had to study the systems of the human body and create a 'map' of those systems.

The students also wrote a story along the lines of an old movie entitled "The Fantastic Voyage." In this story, the student had to save some famous person from some specific malady by miniaturizing themselves and traveling through the celebrity's body. Along the way they had to describe the systems and the organs they encountered. One of my all-time favorites was a story by one young lady who braved the arduous journey to cure President Bush's dislike of broccoli and a chronic vitamin deficiency caused by his refusal to eat the vegetable.

...students design a house and build a scale model of it.

At the second station the students designed a house. Their plan had to include the systems in that house for energy, water, and waste removal. Again they worked in pairs to show how they would adapt their plans to a specific piece of property, and then they had to build a scale model of the house they designed.

In the third and final station, the students worked in small groups to design a plan for our watershed in the year 2020, when they will be the adults in charge. Using all their knowledge of the region, its physical as well its historical aspects, the students had to plan for energy and water distribution, waste water and trash handling, transportation, communication, recreation, and population distribution. Along with an oral presentation of their views of the future, their final report included overlay maps, charts, and plans illustrating the details of these aspects within the watershed.

A complete set of the learning station overviews and descriptions can be found in Appendix F. These are the same documents the students received at the onset of each phase.

During the *Sense of Place* and the *Sense of Time* phases of the year, the students were allowed to work on learning stations at their own pace and in any order they chose. Some, as expected, took readily to this self-controlled learning. Others, also as one would expect, had difficulty disciplining themselves. These latter students found themselves in somewhat of a pressured situation in late November when we approached the deadlines for the *Sense of Place* requirements. The number experiencing similar difficulties toward the end of the *Sense of Time* phase was significantly lower. It seems many students had learned a valuable lesson about time management and responsibility, precisely the lesson we want to teach, but a lesson far too many teenagers do not have an opportunity to learn before they reach college.

For the *Sense of Quality* phase we required the work to be completed in the sequence described: human body, house, watershed regional plan. This because each built logically upon the one or ones before it, outward from the student's own body to his or her house to the region as a whole.

Throughout all the phases, these learning stations were supplemented with other activities. For example, large group reading and discussion sessions each day covered various aspects of the assignments and activities in the stations. This gave students a chance to ask questions, share ideas, and discuss problems. These discussions and readings also ensured that each student confronted all the issues and concepts involved, and gave us a way to gauge their general progress.

We maintained, as we still do, the daily log question. Each day we write a question on the board. This question always pertains to something going on that day, and usually it requires the students to relate and apply information. Students must copy the log question into their log or onto their folder sheet and attempt to answer it for homework. We go over the question and their responses the next morning. Again, this technique provides opportunities to share ideas, to gauge understanding, and to ensure key concepts are confronted.

Other activities we saved from previous years included the "Drip" essay, the "Insects of the Water's Surface" essay, the Create-A-Colony group project, the monthly newsletters and the bimonthly open houses, to name a few.

The last major change we initiated in the fifth year turned out to be one of the most successful. At the end of each phase, the students reviewed what we had covered, then this review was followed by a "Seminar."

The seminar amounted to an oral examination akin to those many of us experienced in college and graduate school. Students in groups of three or four sat for an hour or so with two of the three teachers and discussed the concepts of the phase nearing completion. In small groups of three or four, each student had to participate: no one could hide.

In addition to going over specific facts and answering the students' questions, we asked them questions concerning larger relationships. For example, in the *Sense of Place* seminar we showed the students a certain rock and asked them to take turns telling us anything and everything they could about that rock and its significance to our region. Similarly, in the *Sense of Time* seminar we used a photograph of our local train station. The students' responses to the picture ranged over history, geography, economics, photography, and art. We were amazed and pleased with the quantity and the quality of the students' insights and with their ability to discern and describe sophisticated relationships.

Without the pressure of grades, the students opened up and willingly, gleefully showed us what they had learned and how they could apply that knowledge.

As you can imagine, the students approached the first seminars with a certain degree of trepidation. When the seminars were completed, a process which took several days, the overwhelming student response was, "Can we do them again next week?" The students looked forward to the subsequent seminars. Without the pressure of grades, and in the spirit of cooperative learning, the students opened up and willingly, gleefully showed us what they had learned and how they could apply that knowledge to wider areas. What more could any teacher want?

After Year Five, we again abandoned the learning station format, though we retained the substance as usual. Too many students, we found, neglected to try the optional, blue card activities and focused instead directly on the required ones. As a result, some students missed important opportunities for deeper understanding of complex issues and settled instead for somewhat superficial degrees of comprehension. Furthermore, though we encouraged students to work together on these activities, many students found themselves working in isolation or merely copying someone else's work in their programmed desire to complete required tasks on time—another sad remnant of the "school as factory" mentality already drummed into them.

To avoid these issues, we reworked the stations in three ways: we created problem solving activities which involved the same concepts, we added new group cooperative projects, and we initiated a series of on-going ritualized mini-tasks.

The new problem-solving activities vary in length and complexity. Groups have tackled problem-solving tasks as small as using a topographical map to figure out the actual length of a meandering stream to ones as large as figuring out ways to survey a local pond as part of a real, township sponsored park renovation project.

In addition to these problem-solving activities and the more recognizable remnants of the original WATERSHED plan, we added some new twists to the *Sense of Place*. A favorite of the students is our "Rock Concert" project. Students are required to find a favorite rock on one of their early field study trips. Each student is then placed in a group with students who have selected the same basic type of rock based on the six or seven major rock formations in our region. These groups then research their rock (reminiscent of the original geology report) and visit various locations in the region where that rock type can be found. The group then presents its research to the class in the form of a "Rock Concert," complete with an original rock song and a T-shirt showing where their rock is found.

We also added a Water Fair to the *Sense of Place*. The students had to research everything they could about water. Then they found ways to present the information through entertaining games and activities. One group, for example, constructed a bubble making apparatus to demonstrate principles of water's surface tension.

Another new group activity, this one in *Sense of Time,* involved planning and conducting a Lenape Feast Day. Students arranged themselves in four groups of about ten each. One group planned to teach the rest of us about Lenape games, another group prepared Lenape food and stories to share around a campfire. A third group learned to construct an authentic wigwam and prepared to teach the skills involved to the rest of us. The fourth group worked with various Lenape handicrafts. After researching their topics, the groups got together to organize the feast day using a round-robin type format. Two or three students from a given group, say the game group for example, would stay at their site on the playing field and instruct a group of six to eight students from the other groups. Meanwhile, the rest of the game group visited other activity sites. At prearranged intervals, a different set of presenters would take over and the first set of presenters would visit another group. This procedure gave every student in each group the chance to instruct another group, while also allowing each student the opportunity to visit each of the other presentations.

Activities such as these clearly give students the responsibility for learning concepts and materials in a self-determined, enjoyable way. Faced with this responsibility, and with the added responsibility of having to teach others, students seldom fail. They most often rise to the occasion, create wonderfully unique presentations, and manage to master and retain the concepts involved. Every good teacher knows this, and many good teachers try to accomplish similar activities. We certainly do not mean to claim to have cornered the market on instructional novelty or creativity.

The main point to be emphasized here, however, is that the whole learning structure of WATERSHED allows this type of activity to occur all the time. Often we have multiple activities in various stages of implementation running simultaneously. The classroom teacher in a conventional situation, restricted by departmental concerns and forty-five minute time blocks, faces an overwhelmingly difficult task if he or she wants to implement such an activity. Once again, the problem lies not with the teachers, but with the outmoded system which hinders and often prevents those creative teachers from providing their students with optimal learning experiences of the sort described. Where such experiences do in fact occur, and thankfully they do, the teacher responsible deserves tremendous credit. Unfortunately, such experiences are too few, too isolated—the exception, not the rule.

The third major aspect of restructuring the learning stations involved the creation of on-going mini-tasks. We took many of the optional blue card enrichment activities and made them part of the daily log question procedure, for example. This particular procedure, as explained previously, had existed in one form or another since the beginning of WATERSHED. Students have always been required to keep some sort of log of their daily accomplishments, and the log question has usually been a part of that record. These log questions concern some important aspect of the day's agenda. We go over them the next day to ensure a common base of certain information. The questions also serve as a review of the previous day's work and a lead-in to the present day's planned activities. This serves to provide a sense of structure for each day, a shared starting point from which the students will branch out and sometimes go their separate ways.

To go along with this daily ritual of the log question, we created some weekly activities which provided another level of structure for the students. These included "Microscope Monday," the "Tuesday Task," and "Photographic Friday."

You may recall that microscopy and photography were on-going learning stations in Year Five. The first and last of the three weekly activities just named were designed to present the same skills and concepts, but to ensure that all students took advantage of the opportunity to learn about them. Each Monday the students were presented with a task to accomplish using the microscopes. Early tasks involved learning the parts of the microscope and how to use it properly. Once the technique was mastered, the students faced tasks involving observations. A new slide would be placed under the microscope each Monday, and the students were expected by the following Monday to draw exactly what they observed and to describe it in writing. These slides always enhanced the work we were doing at the time: for example, while working with plants and animals during the *Sense of Place,* the students viewed and described slides of filamentous algae, a euglena, a daphnia, and other organisms we actually find in the streams.

Eventually we added yet another activity to Mondays. It is called "Right Before Your Eyes" based on a series of two page articles by John Weisinger. These short and entertaining articles present interesting information about local plants and animals which we see often but rarely stop to examine closely. The students are asked to read one of these each week, and then we read it aloud as a group and discuss it the following Monday. At the end of the year, we now require each student to imitate Mr. Weisinger's craft by researching and creating a "Right Before My Eyes" about a plant or animal of their own choice. This has become a very popular assignment .

"Photographic Friday" is very similar to "Microscope Monday." Each Friday the students are presented with a task involving photography, and they have until the following Friday to complete that task. At the beginning of the year the students focus their efforts on learning the parts of the SLR camera and how to use it properly. As the year progresses, tasks involve analyzing photographs for elements of composition and technical aspects. Eventually, students learn darkroom techniques as they have to develop and print pictures they have taken. These pictures, while primarily of the students' choosing, include three required photos. Each student must take a portrait of our middle school in the autumn, a portrait of a classmate in the winter, and in the spring a picture which illustrates their personal image of the WATERSHED experience.

The "Tuesday Tasks" represent a weekly opportunity for the students to demonstrate what they have been learning in the past week. The task generally involves writing an essay or story based on an open-ended question concerning relationships we have been studying. This gives us an opportunity, again, for shared experiences, for checking on comprehension, and for working specifically with writing skills. On some occasions throughout the year we change the pace and vary the task to include drawings. One week during *Sense of Place,* for example, we received many clever cartoon versions of the carbon-oxygen cycle. In *Sense of Time* we devote another Tuesday Task to diagraming the parts of a grist mill from the dam through the tailrace. Similarly, the students draw water treatment plant diagrams as a Tuesday Task in *Sense of Quality.*

We round out the week of daily rituals by using Wednesday as our weekly folder day. The students write their self-evaluation and a goal for the coming week. Then we write comments describing each student's activities and accomplishments. Often we attach photos taken during the week so the parents receive a visual as well as a verbal image of their child's work. These folders go home Wednesday afternoon to be signed by the parent and returned on Thursdays.

So, Thursdays, naturally, became "Binder Day." As students bring their weekly folders back and turn in to us their comment sheets, we give them a chance to organize their work in preparation for the coming week. Old work which the parents have now seen is removed from the weekly folder and placed in one of three other locations. Much of the material goes into the student's binder, particularly handout materials, notes, field study data, maps, and so forth. The students organize their binder any way they choose, but they know that they will be called upon at any time to find materials quickly. We also require them to explain their system of binder organization during their first seminar, and we check binders randomly throughout the year to see how the students are maintaining them.

What does not go into the binder is filed in one of two student portfolios, one for written work and one for art work. The writing folder is a working folder which the students use throughout the year as they write and revise essays, letters, stories, and American Diaries. At the end of the year, certain predetermined pieces are transferred to each student's permanent writing folder which follows that student throughout his or her years in Radnor. These predetermined pieces showcase the student's work in various stages of the writing process to demonstrate progress. Each student is also asked to submit his or her favorite piece of writing from the year, along with a brief statement defending that selection and a self-evaluation. The remainder of the working folder and the visual arts folder are returned to the student at the end of the year. Together with the binder, they constitute a wonderful record of the child's year in WATERSHED; a record which many students retain for years after their year with us has ended.

Beyond these weekly rituals, the students also devote class time each week to several long-term projects. These have varied from year to year as the interests of the group have changed. We have had students select current event topics relating to our watersheds and follow these throughout the year. We have had students choose project emphases for the year. For example, some students volunteer to be our hosts and guides for the many visitors who come to the WATERSHED room each year. Others have chosen to work on the canoes, to maintain correspondence with other schools, to conduct acid rain monitoring, to make various videos, or to collate our year-end anthology, just to name a few. In each case, the students work on these project areas at their own pace, or when the need arises, throughout the year. In so doing the students learn and use a wide variety of skills and concepts ranging from artistic skills to public speaking skills to research skills to woodworking skills and everything in between.

As you can see, though Ed and I do very little traditional lecturing in front of the class, there is always plenty of educational work going on. The room may at times look and sound chaotic, but it is a controlled and healthy chaos to which the students respond well and in which most students seem to flourish. Each year since Year Four the new group of students has surpassed their predecessors in both the quantity and the quality of their work. The students never cease to amaze us.

The students never cease to amaze us!

One day, for example, after going over the log question responses and announcing some up-coming project requirements, Ed and I decided to give the students some free work time early in the day. Woody Arnold and our student teacher were taking a group of eight students to a nearby stream research facility to help with a trout egg distribution project. As they were organizing to leave, we let the remaining thirty students begin working on projects and assignments of their own. Some students were finishing topographical maps, some were typing papers on the computers for our newsletter, some were reviewing their videotaped animal reports and writing self-evaluations, some were taping video footage for a documentary on a local stream, some were completing bottom profiles and data summary sheets from a recent field study trip, some were developing film in the darkroom. It was an amazing sight. We planned to pull them together for a reading session after an hour or so, or whenever we felt they were losing momentum. But an hour passed, and they were so diligently working that we opted to let them continue.

Late in the morning, with no direction from us, the students organized a cooperative game and took their snack break. In one sense, this was not too unusual. Because the seventh graders in our school happen to eat during the last lunch session of the day, at 12:15 P.M., the morning is far too long to expect them to survive without food. It is tough for me to go that long; it is particularly difficult for growing twelve year olds accustomed to receiving sustenance on a minute to minute basis! So, we have always permitted and encouraged a healthy snack at some point in the mid-morning. Similarly, we always plan for an organized recess, usually outside, to play cooperative games and to provide those active bodies with exercise and the chance to blow off steam. Again, schools with rigid schedules too often expect of children stamina we would never expect of adults. So, for the students to anticipate these breaks was not at all unusual. The remarkable part was the way they organized the breaks entirely on their own.

Perhaps even more remarkable, twenty minutes later, again without our intervention, they were back to work on their various tasks.

Lunch time came. The students left, though some asked if they could stay in the room and continue working. Half an hour later, back they all came and started working again. Through it all, Ed and I circulated freely to check on progress, to answer questions, to give advice, to make suggestions, and to lend a hand when asked. When our trout egg nesters returned, they joined right in. So passed the day.

We have always permitted a healthy snack...and plan an organized recess.

When it was over, an incredible amount of work and learning had been accomplished. The bin, where students turn in their assignments for us to look at, overflowed with papers, graphs, and drawings. It had been the consummate WATERSHED day, the ideal we strive to have each day, the day which proves it all can work.

Do we have these days every day? Obviously not, though some part of nearly every day fits this description. Nevertheless, we experience the phenomenon with enough frequency to keep us coming in everyday, and to convince us that we could not and would not want to go back to teaching in a traditional classroom or a conventional curriculum.

Over the coming years, we will continue to see changes and to try new strategies within the whole learning philosophy. WATERSHED will continue to form and reform and, with continued good fortune, expand. Through it all, the basic premise with which we started remains and will continue. Students need to feel that they have a place in which they belong, and that they have value; that they have control over and responsibility for their learning. That is their manifest destiny.

In a very real sense, it is our manifest destiny to promote that premise in the hope that others will begin to appreciate it and work toward creating other programs like WATERSHED which embody this philosophy and its methodology.

Place, Time, and Quality 9.

Some three hundred and fifty years after the first Swedes arrived, and more than two hundred years after the last shots were fired at Brandywine or Germantown, our region sits once again on a frontier of sorts. Each of the streams we study begins in semi-rural tranquility but ends in the bustling East Coast megalopolis. In fact, several of the smaller streams run much of their final course channelized through steel or concrete viaducts. So, in one very real sense, this region is on the dividing line between two very different places.

In another equally real sense, this area sits on the frontier between two different times, the past and the future. From this temporal ridge line we can see our world changing from a service economy to an information economy. In turn, we see our communities changing, not just physically, but socially as well, as old forms and definitions breakdown. The isolated communities of my childhood, with recognizable names and boundaries ascribed to their small neighborhoods, playgrounds, and local businesses had become sprawling, nebulous subdivisions by the time I entered college. To shop for clothes, to meet one's friends, or to go to work, one had to drive to the mall or the office complex. Today we are seeing the rise of planned communities with space and energy efficient cluster condominiums, complete with their own mini-malls and office buildings. From one perspective this seems a return to the old communities, but the isolation within these newer communities and the rapid turnover of their populations illustrates an instability not characteristic of the earlier eras. We can bemoan these changes; but we cannot halt them, and we cannot go backwards to bygone eras.

We must go forward; we have no choice. And it is into this new world of accelerating change and instability that we send our students. Yet, we continue to send them out into the 21st century with what amounts to a 19th century education and worldview. Everyday on television, the radio, in magazines and newspapers, we see business and career advertisements which characterize today's and tomorrow's emerging workplaces as ones requiring individuals who possess the skills of teamwork, flexibility, and creativity. We read continually of new participatory management strategies which call upon the workers to take an active role in the decision-making and quality control processes. Yet, our educational system continues to focus narrowly on limited memorization skills, segregated disciplines, short-term views, competition among individuals, and adversarial student-teacher roles.

We do a disservice to our students when we allow the present system to continue even as we recognize its flawed nature.

So, in a very real sense, we sit on a threshold of quality as well. Will we maintain the old, unworkable forms, or will we admit the need for radical changes and implement the necessary moves? On this frontier, I remain somewhat skeptical. As a profession, teaching is admittedly a conservative enterprise. It is to a certain extent necessarily slow to change. The most unconscionable aspect of this however, is the disservice we do to our students when we allow the present system to continue even as we recognize its flawed nature. We know the present educational system is failing in many ways: the traditional, department by discipline approach to middle level learning is no longer adequate. Yet, we resist the change, even when we know how to change for the better.

And we do know that a change toward whole learning strategies will be a change for the better. I have not taken space in these pages to rehash the numerous studies and overwhelming arguments already published which call for change and which support either whole learning and/or co-operative educational strategies. The reader can, if he or she so desires, readily find such documentation from a steadily growing volume of sources.

What is far more significant from my point of view, we know whole learning is a better approach because a program like WATERSHED demonstrates that it works. Despite those who would maintain the status quo, the whole learning approach works for students and their parents.

Whole learning works because it more readily and more fully meets the needs of students and their parents. The students, first and foremost, need a sense of belonging and a sense of self-worth as foundations on which to build the quality of their work and of their thinking. WATERSHED provides for these basic needs in a way that a traditional program simply cannot. The splintered nature of conventional curricula forces students to search elsewhere for a sense of belonging. Fortunate students will find a sense of belonging in some other positive group, perhaps a sports team or a community group. Less fortunate students may find it in a street gang. The whole learning approach, on the other hand, fosters appreciation of quality and the pride of accomplishment, along with giving students a place to belong.

I will never forget this comment made to us by one young lady at the close of her WATERSHED year. She said, "In every other year of school, all I ever had was a locker, but in seventh grade, I had a home."

"In every other year of school, all I ever had was a locker, but in seventh grade, I had a home."

Students also need to see that their learning is interrelated and relevant to their life. Once again, segregated departments, in their very segregation, break down this unity of knowledge. Whole learning seeks to focus on the connections.

Students need to define their learning as a cooperative venture wherein everybody wins only when nobody loses. The whole learning approach fosters this attitude of teamwork and shared responsibility, whereas the traditional approach favors competition and isolation in learning.

Finally, the students need time to experiment with and to absorb learning in an atmosphere of mutual trust and concern. That atmosphere is best achieved when teachers and students have the time to get to know each other by sharing unique and meaningful experiences. A conventional school schedule, broken into discrete forty or forty-five minute segments, cannot adequately provide that time and continuity. WATERSHED does.

Similarly, parents need to feel that their role in the education of their child is a direct role, not an auxiliary one. They need to be players in the process, not spectators. Schools have to reach out in meaningful ways to encourage this parental participation. Too often, traditional school bureaucracies discourage parental involvement. In contrast, the whole learning approach of WATERSHED demands that involvement.

I can only dream about the endless potential of programs such as WATERSHED if and when they can exist without the strain of dealing with the traditional system. I can only imagine how much more we could cover, how much more the students could accomplish, if they entered WATERSHED without the competitive, grade-oriented indoctrination current students have.

Virtually every problem we have experienced in WATERSHED over our seven years is directly connected to one or more conditions caused by the traditional program. We occasionally hear, for example, of a student supposedly having difficulty readjusting to eighth grade. First of all, the mere fact that the students even have to "readjust" is a result of the traditional program which has not yet allowed a follow-up program for WATERSHED students to continue in the whole learning approach. That fact aside, as we probe these situations, we frequently learn that the problem lies less with the students and more with a traditional teacher's inability to accept the student's role as an assertive learner. Often our students will not settle for a mere letter grade on a paper, but will request that their teachers put comments on their work. I have former students every year who bring me their papers in the hope that I will be able to explain the grades given them. Some of my colleagues view this as a challenge to their ability, authority, or integrity, and they treat these students as behavioral problems. Similarly, every year students, and sometimes even their parents, complain to us of teachers who, in essence, have told the student not to ask questions. More than one student has come to us in tears over such incidents.

These active learners will become leaders in the pursuit of knowledge and excellence.

Granted, we, too, pass on students who have still not learned to deal as politely or as tactfully with situations as we would like them to. But generally, the student who sees himself or herself as an active learner will not be the passive, docile receptacle of information many teachers tend to prefer. Instead, these active learners will become leaders in the pursuit of knowledge and excellence. A teacher's job is to guide this pursuit, not impede it.

Another problem our students face stems from their continuing identity as a group, or at least from other peoples' perceptions of that identity. As opposed to being a nameless student in the general mass, WATERSHED students are instantly recognized. This sense of belonging, of identity is inherently good for the children, as we have shown. On the other hand, no one knows a student as a 7A'er or a 7B'er. Those team members have no real identity, which is too bad, as we have noted. The identity that WATERSHED students have, however, is sometimes used against them. Ten students can be making noise in the hallway, for example; if only one is a WATERSHED student, he or she is recognized, and the blame for the entire situation, rightly or wrongly, often falls on WATERSHED.

The reader may be inclined to think this mere paranoia on my part, but I have seen such instances occur frequently over the last seven years. In an analytical way, I understand the reasons behind it. WATERSHED, or any other viable alternative program, represents a tangible threat to the establishment and to those with a vested interest in that existing system. Indeed, the whole learning approach advocated here openly calls for the dissolution of the conventional system. In the face of that threat, adherents of the traditional philosophy will actively seek ways to discredit the alternative and thus justify their continued existence.

As a case in point, I remember quite vividly a conversation I had with a high school teacher friend of mine during the year our first WATERSHED students were ninth graders. He complained that the freshmen class was the worst that the high school had seen in years. He went on to blame it on the non-traditional methods and attitudes we advocate in WATERSHED. I pressed him for names of those students he felt were the negative influences in the class. He quickly fired off ten or twelve names of those students he thought to be the worst offenders: those he thought showed little desire to learn anything, and who were openly insubordinate to the teachers. Not one of the students he named had been in WATERSHED. I then asked him to identify class leaders. Another ten or so names came up: many of these had been WATERSHED participants.

The exact same thing happened again just this past year. This time an eighth grade "specials" teacher complained about students and accused us of not doing enough to prepare the WATERSHED students for their return to the conventional program in eighth grade. Again I asked for names. Again most of the names I was given were not WATERSHED students. Still, somehow, WATERSHED often gets the blame.

Our students face a similar set of disparaging and erroneous attitudes from their peers. Every year from the very first, usually around mid-November or so, the WATERSHED students come to us and complain that they are falling behind the other seventh graders and will not be adequately prepared for eighth grade. When asked how they determined this, the students reveal that this is what they are being told by those other students. We have already shown that WATERSHED students do not fall behind; in fact, they tend to be better prepared in several ways—a fact almost any past WATERSHED student will gladly confirm. Yet, every year our students have to be reassured that their "friends" are mistaken. In many cases these other students may be speaking from ignorance or to some extent from jealousy. After all, most of the students who try to denigrate the WATERSHED program are the same ones who wanted to be in it but were not selected by the computer. Their sour grapes reaction is predictable and understandable. Nevertheless, the WATERSHED students must deal with it.

Beyond the prevalence of these attitudes and misconceptions, the whole learning method faces a much greater challenge in the form of obstacles continually thrown in its path. Recall, for example, the pilot evaluation in which we were required to go back over our whole learning activities and segregate content areas and skills. In a similar fashion, Ed and I are frequently required to follow procedures designed to accommodate the large teams. We are required, for example, to sit through meetings at which the other teams debate their various problems with student behavior, parent communications, planning, grading, and so forth; problems we do not have in WATERSHED. Little changes as a result of these meetings, so these procedures and meetings are wasteful and inefficient; particularly to a two-person team such as ours which shares the same room, is in continuous communication, and employs the whole learning methodology. If an entire school were arranged using the whole learning model, few if any of these procedures or meetings would be necessary at all. Much more time and energy could be directed where it truly belongs, toward the students. Yet, even as we witnessed with the outside evaluation teams' recommendations, the other teams apparently cannot recognize this. They view our suggestions as irrelevant, even though we can demonstrate conclusively that the whole learning approach eliminates many of the very issues with which they are grappling at these meetings.

So, where do we go from here? Acknowledging the need for change, and providing an example of a way to change, how do we implement change. How do we spread the whole learning philosophy?

Everywhere Ed and I go, everywhere we speak about WATERSHED, audiences recognize the potential of the whole learning approach as we embody it. They openly express their admiration and support for programs of this sort. However, each and every time we address an audience we also hear the lament, "But we can't do that here."

I maintain that they can do it, and they can do it anywhere. All the arguments, all the impediments, all the negative conditions we hear used to excuse inaction are ones we have confronted and successfully overcome. We have yet to hear of an obstacle so substantial that it could not be removed if a given faculty had the determination and the drive to implement the alternatives we suggest. WATERSHED's very existence attests to the unlimited possibilities; and every year WATERSHED continues to thrive strengthens this position, while weakening the arguments against whole learning curricula.

How can we make radicals out of conservatives without scaring them away?

Given that many would like to work in whole learning situations but are not perhaps willing or prepared to risk their time, effort, or careers fighting for such programs, how can we help them move in the right direction? How can we make radicals out of conservatives without scaring them away? Clearly several issues and strategies must be addressed simultaneously.

First, on the governmental level, states have to rethink their respective teacher certification requirements. Instead of focusing on a subject area of expertise, as they do now, certification requirements ought to emphasize excellence across a broad spectrum of subject areas. Prospective teachers should be required to demonstrate their abilities to integrate disparate concepts. No teacher should be certified in science, for example, who can not communicate effectively and show children how to write effectively. No teacher should be certified in language arts without a strong background in areas to which those language arts are applied, areas such as science and social studies.

Better yet, state certification by subject area could be abandoned altogether. A new middle level certification could be created. This new certification would prepare the next generation of teachers directly in the whole learning philosophy and techniques. These future teachers could be required to design whole learning programs, and they should student teach in whole learning programs to see how their ideas can become reality. This, in turn, means we need more whole learning programs at both the secondary and the collegiate levels.

The greatest key to success, however, rests on the local level. School district administrators must be willing to allow—indeed, to encourage—more flexibility and creativity from the teachers, much as large industries are doing with their workers. Administrative leadership must be willing to look at alternative scheduling and staffing configurations which focus on the needs of the students and which allow teachers the latitude to meet those needs without so many bureaucratic hindrances. Experimental, alternative programs can be initiated, much as WATERSHED was at first, using interested teachers—and there are many such teachers out there. Administrators must be willing to give these teachers the support and the help they need to get programs started. Once past the administrative hurdles, the actual development of a whole learning program is relatively easy. Once other teachers see just how rewarding it is, more and more will be willing to try whole learning programs—if they know they will receive the necessary administrative support.

School district administrators must be willing to allow—indeed to encourage—more flexibility and creativity from teachers.

Just as critical, teachers' unions and associations also must put the needs of the students ahead of their own needs. They need to rethink contract issues such as planning time, certification restrictions, and departmental tunnel vision which often work against the most efficient use of time and personnel resources. There are ways to maintain many of the worthwhile benefits of teaching as a profession without sacrificing the quality of the educational service we provide. Too often union leaders seem to lose sight of this fact. A retooled educational system does not necessarily mean a reduction in force, just as it does not necessarily require an increase in staff levels. It merely requires a rethinking of the nature of the teaching job and a willingness on the part of teachers to redefine and expand their own personal limits. No good teacher need fear change to whole learning programs. I believe most would truly relish the opportunity to try it and would flourish in it—if, again, they know they have administrative support and community consensus.

After all, whole learning offers teachers a chance to develop a program based in part on their own interests. Ed and I started with our love for canoeing. Such a venture can be a truly exciting opportunity to grow as a person and as a teacher, while at the same time providing a better learning environment for the students.

Whole learning properly implemented, is a win-win situation for all concerned.

Finally, parents need to be more proactive. They should talk with their school board representatives, administrators, and teachers. They can tell them about whole learning and encourage them to learn more about programs such as WATERSHED. If a parent finds a sympathetic ear, give that administrator or teacher all the encouragement and support possible. By so doing, parents can improve the educational system for children everywhere as they become true partners in education. To my way of thinking, whole learning, when properly constructed and implemented, is a win-win situation for all concerned.

Is all this too much to ask? Perhaps. There are times when I question whether or not things will ever change. There are many days when I grow frustrated and wonder why I am even bothering to write this book. I know from first-hand experience that many will think the effort futile; others will think it crazy. Still others will continue to bury their heads and claim that the present system works just fine.

Yet, I also recognize that change is imminent. Perhaps not as radical in nature nor as rapid as I would like; but change is coming nonetheless. Many of these same issues, for example, are already being addressed as more and more states have begun looking at a new philosophy of outcome-based education and competency based graduation requirements to replace the Carnegie unit philosophy of graduating students for time served. Whole learning strategies are custom made for this new type of philosophy. As more states approve versions of this performance based system, whole learning programs arranged around any number of possible topics will become easier to propose and to implement.

In a similar vein, large school districts facing increasing violence among students might well resort to metal detectors and dictatorial discipline codes to enforce behavior through fear. Or, these districts might stop reinforcing the message that might makes right and turn instead to building respect and cooperation through whole learning. Smaller learning communities designed around the WATERSHED whole learning model could help create more positive, certainly less hostile learning environments. Such programs have the true potential to build more stable, personalized relationships among students and teachers. These whole learning programs can provide a sense of identity for students which, in turn, can increase their self-esteem. This then increases their sense of pride in their work. Better relationships of this sort yield greater levels of student achievement while reducing the negative factors which breed discipline problems and disruptions to the learning process. Nothing encourages success like success, and whole learning offers students a greater chance for that success.

Along this same line, offering a wide variety of whole learning programs would further enhance the students' chances for success. When we allow students' interest to drive the curriculum, rather than outmoded predetermined single subject concerns, the students will respond with greater enthusiasm for learning which translates directly into greater achievement.

The bottom line:

- **smaller communities of learners are better than larger ones;**

- **hands-on, experiential learning is better than second-hand, textbook learning;**

- **an atmosphere of mutual respect and trust promotes learning better than does an atmosphere of fear and mistrust.**

In short, the whole learning approach, as demonstrated in WATERSHED is a better way to structure our educational system for the 21st century than is the departmentalized structure currently in use. The time has come to abandon the outmoded system based on 19th century factory needs and adopt a system geared to prepare our students to function on the information superhighway.

129

Can it happen? Despite daily vacillations, I remain optimistic. Looking at the big picture, I know change will come. There will always be individuals out there willing to fight or subvert the bureaucracy. True, there will always be doubters, reactionaries who hope somehow to push back the clock to some simpler time. There will always be the dreamless dead, but there will always be those as well who possess the creativity, sense of humor, and common sense to create a fresh program when the need exists but the system makes no provision for one. There will always be daring and resilient explorers willing to confront the frontiers of place, time, and quality and to push those boundaries further into the future.

Can it happen? It has to happen. One way or another, rivers always find their way to the sea.

Epilogue

She appeared from nowhere as she always does—rising from the river's edge, her great wings lifting her slender body silently, effortlessly over the sparkling water. The Native Americans called her "the spirit guide/the one who shows the way." She rounded the bend leading us down the river with an unhurried grace that was to characterize our educational journey.

The magical appearance of a Great Blue Heron was a sign. The students expressed their surprise and pleasure at the sight. Mark and I smiled as we marched the forty seventh graders across the flood plain to their first encounter with the lovely east branch of the Brandywine River. The Great Blue told us we were on the right path, we were in the right place, we had made the right decision. WATERSHED was going to work if we continued to listen to our students, focus on the stream, and follow the Great Blue.

Now, almost seven years later, we have felt the joy of discovery, the wonder of truly integrated curriculum, and the excitement of a new way of learning. Each year the saga continues as our students take wing on their educational journey following the path of the stream and the "spirit guide."

—Ed Silcox

References

Delaware County Intermediate Unit 25, K-12 Science Program Evaluation Team (1991, March 12-14). Radnor Township School District Evaluation Summary Report.

Hassler, Robert (1994). The Effect of Various Curricular Delivery Systems on the Academic Achievement, Self-Concept, Attendance, and Behavior of Seventh Grade Students. Unpublished doctoral dissertation. Lehigh University.

Jacobson, Cliff (1987, May). Classroom in Canoes. *Canoe Magazine, XV,* pp. 28-32.

Kolman, Peter S. et al. (1992, June). The Outside Team Evaluation Report for Radnor Middle School.

Weisinger, John (1987). "Right Before Your Eyes," Natural History Mini-Poster Series.

The Original Proposal

The following document outlines the original alternative program as we envisioned it. This document was written in January of 1986 and submitted to the Radnor Board of School Directors in February of that same year.

PROFESSIONAL DEVELOPMENT PLAN:

AN ALTERNATIVE LEARNING PROGRAM

Submitted by

Ed Silcox and Mark Springer

PURPOSE

Our goal is to develop an alternative curricular structure which can cover traditional skills and concepts through a holistic combination of classroom and on-site learning experiences.

RATIONALE

Given the myriad differences in individual students' learning styles and abilities, it is apparent that no single curricular structure can satisfy all needs. Alternative forms of curricula are advisable to help meet this variety of needs.

In the pursuit of our Professional Development Plan, we believe that we have found such an alternative. As structured it will provide students with a different, yet equally excellent educational experience at an efficient cost.

DESCRIPTION

Approximately forty (40) randomly selected seventh grade students representing all ability levels would be grouped together under the direction of two full-time teachers of science and English and one part-time teacher of mathematics.

This group would devote its _entire_ school year, all day / every day, to the comprehensive examination of a specific watershed; and the skills and concepts taught in the traditional disciplines would be focused on this river study. The Brandywine River would be the first to be studied because it is rich in historical, cultural, industrial and geographical significance; because it is wholly and readily accessible; and because support services are immediately available to us. Should this program become a reality, other watersheds would be examined in other years. Again, however, it is important to note that regardless of the particular watershed examined, all the conventional seventh grade areas of study would be incorporated into the investigation: English, math, science, social studies, humanities, reading, art, music and physical education would all be included.

The classroom activities would involve:

— learning to conduct laboratory tests on water, soil and air samples;
— studying the physics of the river's flow and its effects on the surrounding landscape;
— identifying the plants and animals inhabiting the watershed;
— researching the river's role in the agriculture, industry, history and artistic culture of the region;
— analyzing topographical, planning and geo-political maps of the area, and looking for interrelationships depicted;
— learning the first aid, safety and canoeing skills needed for safe river exploration; and
— examining the students' personal role in the future as members of a watershed community.

Field trips and guest speakers would enhance these classroom experiences. Trips would include visits to:

— the Brandywine Valley Association Center,
— the Chester County Historical Society,
— the Brandywine River Museum,
— the Chester County Library,
— the Brandywine Battlefield,
— the Hagley Museum,
— historical buildings along the river, e.g., old mills or the Chad House, etc.,
— local farms and local industries,
— Chester County governmental and public works agencies,
    and others as yet undetermined.

Similarly, guest speakers might include:

— Mrs. Jeanine LaRouche on Oral History,
— Mr. Andrew Wyeth or Mr. George Weymouth on Brandywine Arts,
— Mr. William Baldwin, authority on Chester County history,
— Mr. Dick James on weather and ecology,
— Dr. Dale Springer on local geology,
— Ms. Polly Johnsen on aquatic biology,
— and as yet undetermined professors from local colleges, representatives of local industries, governmental officials, Red Cross instructors in first aid and/or safety, and numerous Brandywine Valley Association personnel with various areas of expertise.

In addition to the above, as much time as possible would be spent on the river. Walking and / or canoeing its entire length in a series of outings, the students would put to practical and first-hand use the skills acquired in the classroom. They would, for example, measure and map selected portions of the river; perform chemical, physical and biotic measurement tests; observe and describe the flora and fauna encountered; and then record all of their results, observations, experiences, and reactions in writing, art, and film.

By the end of the year-long program the students would collate all of their work in book form. Ideally publishable, this record would be a unique description of the watershed in all its facets, including its physical, geographical, biological, ecological, historical, sociological and cultural aspects. It would also be a worthwhile contribution to our community-at-large, as well as a tangible product in which the students could feel a sense of true pride and accomplishment.

INITIAL SUPPORT RESOURCES

The Brandywine Valley Association, (BVA), the oldest small watershed association in America, has expressed an active interest in cooperating with Radnor in the establishment of this program. Their director, Mr. Robert Struble, and their naturalist/educator, Ms. Ann Faulds, will work closely with us as we write the specific lesson plans and design activities—some of which they have asked us to pilot in a BVA summer program. They will advise us on appropriate strategies and locations, provide us with access to the river, and put us in contact with innumerable sources for field trips and guest speakers. BVA personnel will also help us locate materials, plan trips and develop specific projects. They have offered to accompany us on some of our excursions along the river, and to help the students conduct tests and establish beneficial conservation projects.

In return, we will write the applicable portions of our curriculum in a form which BVA can subsequently use with other school districts in their continuing education programs, and perhaps as a model for Pennsylvania's mandated environmental education program as well. Furthermore, our cooperative efforts will enable BVA to seek foundation and governmental funding for certain expenses pertaining to the project—funding which could at least indirectly cut costs for Radnor.

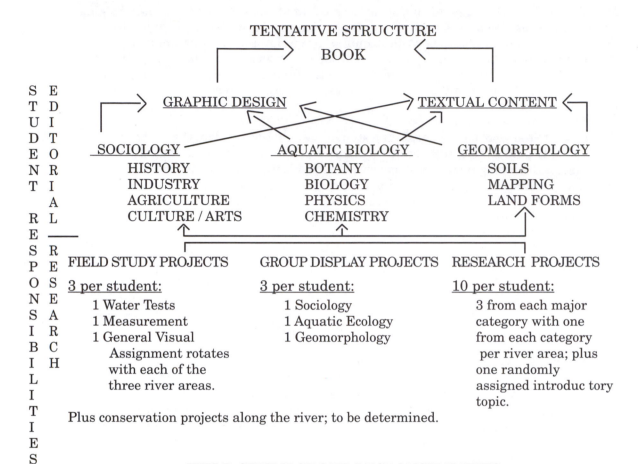

TENTATIVE STRUCTURE
BOOK

GRAPHIC DESIGN   TEXTUAL CONTENT

SOCIOLOGY	AQUATIC BIOLOGY	GEOMORPHOLOGY
HISTORY	BOTANY	SOILS
INDUSTRY	BIOLOGY	MAPPING
AGRICULTURE	PHYSICS	LAND FORMS
CULTURE / ARTS	CHEMISTRY	

S **E**
T **D**
U **I**
D **T**
E **O**
N **R**
T **I**
  A
R **L**
E
S **R**
P **E**
O **S**
N **E**
S **A**
I **R**
B **C**
I **H**
L
I
T
I
E
S

FIELD STUDY PROJECTS	GROUP DISPLAY PROJECTS	RESEARCH PROJECTS
3 per student:	3 per student:	10 per student:
1 Water Tests	1 Sociology	3 from each major
1 Measurement	1 Aquatic Ecology	category with one
1 General Visual	1 Geomorphology	from each category
Assignment rotates		per river area; plus
with each of the		one randomly
three river areas.		assigned introduc tory
		topic.

Plus conservation projects along the river; to be determined.

FIELD STUDY GROUP RESPONSIBILITIES

1. <u>WATER TESTS</u>:

    A.   pH, O2, CO2, Nitrates, Phosphates
    B.   Biotic Index
    C.   Turbidity
    D.   Temperature

2. MEASUREMENTS:

    A.   Depth, width, volume
    B.   Gradient
    C.   Velocity
    D.   Discharge
    E.   Directions
    F.   Distances

3. <u>GENERAL VISUAL</u>:

    A.   Vegetation
    B.   Animals seen
    C.   Overt signs of erosion, conservation, etc.
    D.   Gross Description of Section: Structures, Usage, etc.
    E.   Photographs and Drawings of the section.

SAMPLE GROUP DISPLAY PROJECTS

— Mineral collections with topographical map to pinpoint locations

— Insect collections with charts of maturation stages

— Working model of a mill with undershot wheel

— Model of Lenni-Lenape village and fishing seines

— Three-dimensional topographical map of the watershed

— Stream table to demonstrate flow characteristics or biotics

— Chart of concerned governmental agencies and their responsibilities

— Pictorial timeline of historical and cultural events

— Photographic record of the course

— Slide-tape presentation of any specific aspect of the study

— Photographs of erosion/conservation

— Map overlays showing changes in sub-urbanization

— Leaf/seed collections

— Core samples of soils with analyses

— Charts of canoe parts, strokes, safety, etc.

— Graphs of population growth and density with maps to illustrate why growth occurs in certain areas

— Multi-media presentations of arts of the Brandywine

— Pictorial overview of architectural changes

— Pictorial essay on trash/waste cycle with effects on river ecology

— Seasonal changes in the river's milieu: a photographic overview

— Famous people of the area and their contributions

— Model of early Swedish settlements

SAMPLE INDIVIDUAL RESEARCH PROJECTS

I. SOCIOLOGY:

- Famous people: Wyeths, Pyle, Schoonover, Hesselius, DuPonts, etc.
- Landmarks: buildings, bridges, railroads, roads, etc.
- Placename etymologies
- Literature of the area
- Indians of the area
- Specific local industries: DuPont, Lukens, Schramm, etc.
- Local legends, customs, etc.
- Municipal services
- Transportation: roads, railroads, etc.
- Historical documents pertaining to the area.
- Growth of specific towns: Coatesville, Downingtown, Wilmington, etc.
- Local industries and their connection with the river
- Local government: history and/or legislation regarding the river
- The Brandywine School of Art
- Earliest settlements
- Agriculture of the area
- Historical events occurring in the area
- Modern identity of the area

II. AQUATIC ECOLOGY:

- Specific animals inhabiting the region: numerous possibilities
- Specific plants of the region: numerous possibilities
- Properties of water
- The water cycle
- Flood control
- Erosion/conversation in the area
- Waste removal in the area
- Acid rain and its effects

III. GEOMORPHOLOGY:

- Paleo-history of the region
- Physiological provinces
- Geological maps
- Mineral/soil-type distributions and their relation to agriculture and industry

Summer Packet

The following section presents parts of the most recent Summer Packet we distribute annually in June to the next year's class. Though there have been changes in these packets over the years, they have remained basically the same. For the sake of space, I have not included items that change each year such as the list of participants or the maps and pictures we use. Some of these latter elements would be difficult to reproduce in this context. Nor are reprints of the various articles we ask students to read. Their titles, however, should give the reader a clear sense of what they are about and why they would be in the summer packet. Included are those articles written by our own students. Each year we replace another "professional" article with one written by the students. The September calendar is intended as a sample. Though similar, it would not be the same each year.

Dear _____

    Welcome to WATERSHED!!

    Though the next school year may seem a long way off, and no one wants to rush the summer vacation away, September will be here before we know. We are very excited about the coming year, and we hope you are, too.

    To help you prepare, we're giving you this packet of materials and information which we hope you'll find useful. Please read through these materials carefully and complete the various assignments. They are designed to give you a head start on your work so we can get right into our stream testing in the autumn. Let us know if you have any questions or problems. Feel free to contact us at school if we can be of any assistance.

    Have a safe, happy and relaxing summer! Let us hear from you!

Mark Springer
Ed Silcox
Woody Arnold

ENCLOSED: List of participants
                 Tentative calendar for September
                 List of materials you will need
                 Map assignments
                 Vocabulary assignment
                 Keys for biotic indexing / suggested activity / assignment
                 Questions for the reading assignments
                 Reading assignments:
                          "The Water Cycle," "Dissolved Oxygen," "The Cold War," "Water sheds and You," "Ivy's Oily Resin," Letters and advice from the WATERSHED Class of 1992 - 93, Postcard

September 1993

WELCOME TO WATERSHED

Sunday	Monday	Tuesday	Wednesday	Thursday	Friday	Saturday
			1	2	3	4
5	6 Labor Day	7	8	9 WELCOME to WATERSHED	10	11
12	13 Gulph Creek Walk 1 Open House	14	15 Gulph Creek Walk 2	16 Rosh Hashanah: No School	17 Gulph Creek Walk 3	18
19	20 Fenimore: Field Study, Canoeing	21	22 Fenimore: Field Study, Canoeing	23	24 Canoe Trip Schuylkill River	25
26	27	28 First Field Study Van Trips	29 First Folder Day	30 Field Study Van Trips		

140

SOME LETTERS TO YOU FROM THE WATERSHED CLASS OF 1992-93

Dear Future Watersheders,

   You are in for a great experience that you will remember forever. It is called Watershed. In this year-long project you will learn about the area in which we live: its history, its positive traits, its negative traits, and most of all where it is located relative to everything else in the world. One day you might learn about a nearby creek, and the next day learn about foreign customs.

   One great advantage to Watershed is that not only do the two teachers teach us, but we also teach each other. You will be comfortable by the end of the year with standing in front of large groups and finding interesting ways of presenting information.

   Another great thing that I think you will enjoy about Watershed is the many field trips we take in our area and beyond. Field study trips are trips to local streams where we test the water both physically and chemically and discover if the stream is healthy or not. You will learn about the different animals that live in the streams, and what their habitats are. You will understand how important our area is and what we can do to help it stay that way. In Watershed you will be involved in many types of organizations, including environmental ones.

   Overall, Watershed may be a lot of work, but it is worth the experience. I hope you have as great a time as I did in this truly special program.
                              Sincerely, Tracy J.

Dear Next Year's Watershed Class:

   I am very happy that you are going to have the opportunity I'm having in Watershed. This is a chance to work and have fun at the same time. Next year you will be going on a series of field trips. The trips are fun, but you also have to work hard. If you go on these trips thinking it's not a lot of work, you're in for a big disappointment. On these trips you have to conduct a series of chemical and physical tests. These tests help you understand more about the stream and your "watershed." You also get to look for many bugs and critters in the stream. The more you participate on these trips, the more you will learn, and the better you will do when you get back to school. You will also go on class and family canoe trips. These are lots of fun and hard work.

   Back in the classroom you will be very busy with projects, reports and using your time to make Watershed memorable to you. During class you have to plan your time very carefully. Since you don't have periods, you have all day to work and catch up on assignments. It is important to plan your time and not talk with friends all day, or you will find yourself behind in the projects. Even though you don't get a grade in Watershed, you should take responsibility for your work.

   But the greatest thing about Watershed is the experience you gain. I think it is so fun and cool to get taught by your teachers in school and then go experience it outside the next day. I never really understood what teachers used to teach me, until now that I can relate to it in the real world. Besides, learning outside is so much fun. I haven't had this much fun on field trips in the longest time.

   I am so glad that I was accepted into Watershed. I think every kid and grown-up in the world should get to be in Watershed and learn about the streams near them. I think you are very lucky to be one of the kids to have this great experience.
                              Alexandra N.

Dear Future Watersheders,

Watershed is definitely an opportunity that you don't want to miss out on. I will give you a few tips about making the beginning of seventh grade a great one. The whole concept of Watershed is that you can be involved in learning, and not just sit there for forty-five minutes with a textbook. Watershed is hands-on experience in streams and many other places.

During the Sense of Place unit you will be studying certain streams and finding out how to do different tests there. Don't worry if you don't catch on right away, because trust me, it will all come to you. You will get many opportunities to show off your writing; but if you're nervous, there's no reason to be. The teachers will help you improve tremendously.

There are so many trips to look forward to that I just can't describe them all. Throughout the Sense of Time you will learn about the people who lived in our area long ago. It is very interesting. You will write about your experiences as if you were those people. Sense of Time is the longest unit, but there's so much to do.

In the last section of the year, Sense of Quality, you will learn about the human body, make house designs, and you will go back to the streams. This unit is so great because you do so many different things.

If you ever need help or advice in anything, don't be afraid to ask either one of the teachers. That's what I did at first, and I regret it now because it would've helped me get over my shyness earlier. They are more than willing to help out.

What we call the five C's are very important to abide by. They are Cooperation, Caution, Caring, Courage and Commitment. They may sound a bit corny, but you will later realize how valuable they are. Cooperation is so important because you need to be able to depend on each other and learn how to work together. It is very important to be cautious on trips because some of the trips are very dangerous. You will be fine as long as you use lots of caution. You need to care about other peoples' feelings and their materials. It is important that you think about what you say and do before you actually do it. You should never go out on a field study trip (or any trip) being pessimistic about things. You should be optimistic! If you have lots of courage, you'll be great! You are committed to the program for the whole year of seventh grade. Once you're in, you can't back down. Also, you are committed to hand in all your work at top quality, even if it means it will be a day or two late.

This is a chance to meet some new people. I can guarantee that you will make some very close friends. You might want to sit with different people every so often. You never know, maybe everyone you thought had cooties doesn't.

If you ever need some advice about Watershed, you can ask one of us.

Get yourselves pumped for a fabulous year in Watershed. We hope you have as much fun as we did!

Kim S.

THINGS YOU WILL NEED

I. IN CLASS: Approximately 140 of our days together will be spent at school, where we will be involved in a wide variety of activities. Any special or unusual materials will be provided for you. There are, however, a few items you should acquire and have with you in class each day, right from day #1.

   A. A sturdy three-ring binder in which you will be keeping all the handouts and all your finished assignments

   B. Three (3) 8" x 11" spiral notebooks, each with at least 200 sheets of paper. Print your name clearly on the front and back cover of each notebook. Label one notebook MATH, one NOTES, and one RESEARCH. The latter two notebooks should be multi-subject notebooks.

   C. One smaller stenographer's notebook to take on trips

   D. One good 9" x 12" sketchbook

   E. Pencils and pens for writing, and a set of colored pencils for drawing

   F. A free reading book

   G. You may also need the following useful items to keep handy in your desk: scissors, scotch tape, white out, a stapler, a ruler, a set of markers, and white glue.

II. FOR FIELD STUDY TRIPS: We will spend about 25 days during the year at the streams. On each of these days, regardless of the weather, you will get WET! So, BE PREPARED ! We require that you bring the following items on each trip:

   A. Old sneakers for wading in the water. (you never know what objects may be lurking on the stream bottom!)
       (NOTE: Shoes must tie: slip-ons are not safe. So save those old camp/ summer sneakers !)

   B. A swimsuit, usually worn under your clothes

   C. Old clothes you don't mind getting wet. We recommend an old sweatshirt, jeans or shorts (depending on the weather) and socks

   D. A complete change of clothes to be left back at school or on the bus. Remember: being wet increases the chances of hypothermia (getting too cold). Dry clothes are important!

E. At least one towel. (Please make sure all articles are clearly marked with your name ! !)

F. On some trips you will need to bring your lunch. Please bring your lunch in double plastic bags. Avoid any glass containers, and keep trash to a minimum. You are responsible for your trash ! We recommend that you consider investing in reusable plastic containers. You might wish to bring a snack for the bus ride, too!

G. A water resistant bag to carry all of the above.

Please leave all valuables at home. If you have contact lenses, glasses or retainers, please carry an appropriate case or container with you on all trips.

Please remember: no matter where we go, be it a stream or a museum, YOU represent Radnor, WATERSHED, your Parents and Yourself. We will expect you to be the best that you can be at all times   -   Cooperative, Responsive and Polite.

The most important thing that you need to bring each day is a

POSITIVE ATTITUDE ! !

A series of maps would follow at this point. They include a map of the United States, one of Pennsylvania, one of southeastern Pennsylvania, and one of the particular watershed(s) we are focusing on that year. Students must locate directions and important features on each of these maps in increasing levels of specificity and detail.

WATERSHED   SUMMER VOCABULARY LIST   NAME:_____

When you arrive in September, we will expect you to KNOW these important terms which we will be using throughout the year. Please write a definition IN YOUR OWN WORDS for each term and use each in an appropriate sentence.

Aquatic:

Biotic:

Contour:

Effluent:

Geography:

Geology:

Habitat:

Infiltration (as pertaining to ground water):

Larva/nymph:

Photosynthesis:

Precipitation:

Riffle:

Topography:

Tributary:

Watershed:

Name: _____

Please answer the following questions based on your reading of the articles enclosed. We will collect your answers on the first day of school in September.

1. In your own words, explain the difference between Class I and Class III organisms for biotic indexing.

2. Describe at least two ways water changes as it goes through the hydrologic (water) cycle.

3. Describe at least three conditions that can effect the amount of Dissolved Oxygen in a stream.

4. In your own words, what is a watershed?

5. List three interesting facts about fresh water and how we use it.

6. What are two ways people affect watersheds?

The articles and illustrations that would be included here describe the process of biotic indexing, how to identify benthic invertebrates, the water cycle, dissolved oxygen, poison ivy, the concept of a watershed and how we use fresh water. There is also a brief article explaining that one does not catch a cold by being cold—a common misconception. I am including here only those written by our students, one on the water cycle and one about dissolved oxygen.

THE WATER CYCLE   by Lynette W.
                                                   1991 - 92

Water . . .

It's everywhere.

We drink it; we swim in it; we wash in it; we even breathe it.

Water . . .

It's essential to all life on earth.

How come we never run out? After four and one half billion years you'd think the water would be all used up! It's not, though, and all because of one special process, the HYDROLOGIC CYCLE, more commonly called "the Water Cycle."

This Hydrologic Cycle recycles the earth's valuable water supply. In other words, the water keeps getting reused over and over. Just think, the next glass of water you drink could have been part of a dinosaur's bath in the Mesozoic Era one hundred million years ago, then been frozen in a glacier for thousands of years, and then been boiled to make steam for a generator at the PECO power plant! That glass of water has been a liquid, a solid, and a gas countless times over thanks to the water cycle.

The energy that powers this remarkable process is, of course, the Sun. The sun's energy in the form of light, heat and wind causes water to EVAPORATE from oceans, rivers, lakes and even puddles. "Evaporate" means it turns the water from a liquid to a gas, or "vapor." Warm air currents rising from the earth's surface lift this water vapor up into the atmosphere.

When the air currents reach the cooler layers of the atmosphere, the water vapor condenses around and clings on to fine particles in the air. This step is called CONDENSATION. When enough vapor attaches itself to tiny pieces of dust, pollen or pollutants, it forms a cloud. Clouds do not last forever. Old clouds constantly re-evaporate and new ones form creating ever-changing patterns in the sky.

As the air gets more and more moist, the droplets that form the clouds will grow larger and larger. Eventually they will get so big that the swirling atmospheric winds can no longer hold them up. The droplets then fall from the sky as PRECIPITATION. Precipitation can be in the form of rain, snow, sleet or hail depending on other atmospheric conditions such as temperature.

Once the precipitation reaches the ground, several things can happen to it. First, it might be re-evaporated: we've all seen the mist rising off hot roads after a summer shower. If it isn't re-evaporated, much of the water will become RUN-OFF forming streams and rivers flowing back into the ocean.

Some of the precipitation will be absorbed into the ground. This is called INFILTRA-TION. Once in the ground, the water can join the earth's GROUND WATER supply. This is one of the world's largest storehouses of water. The water could also be absorbed from the ground by the roots of plants.

If plants take in the water, it will become part of the PHOTOSYNTHESIS / RESPIRA-TION cycle in the plants' cells. In PHOTOSYNTHESIS the plants use water and carbon dioxide to make food, called GLUCOSE, a type of simple sugar. In RESPIRATION, this glucose is then used by the plants (and by everything that eats plants) as energy for growth. During both photosynthesis and respiration some water is left over or given off as a waste. This water is given off through the leaves of plants or through the pores and breath of animals. Check out your own breath on a cold day: that's water vapor being given off by your body. We call this TRANSPIRATION, and it is another form of evapora-tion.

With transpiration and evaporation, the cycle begins again: EVAPORATION, CONDEN-SATION, PRECIPITATION, RUN-OFF, INFILTRATION, and TRANSPIRATION. Each time a molecule of water goes through the cycle it is cleaned, or purified, so it can be used by plants and animals again tomorrow, next year, and hopefully forever.

The WATER CYCLE   (based on a drawing by Alison S.)

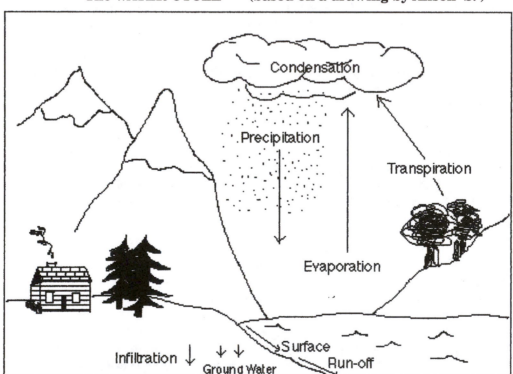

DISSOLVED OXYGEN   by Leily Lajevardi
                                                    1992 - 93

You probably know what would happen to us if we had no oxygen: we would die. Well, animals in the stream need oxygen to live, too. As we all know, water has oxygen in in (H20), but the critters in the stream can't use the oxygen that makes up the water. That's where dissolved oxygen comes along. Dissolved Oxygen, or D.O. for short, is unbound or loose molecules of oxygen that are available for the animals the stream to breathe through their gills.

How does dissolved oxygen get into the water? A good question. There are three ways it gets there. The first way is called aeration. This is a physical process where water running over rocks captures oxygen from the air. The second way is through diffusion. This is a process similar to aeration, but it happens even in still water. It is the mixing of air with water wherever their surfaces come into contact with each other. The water pulls oxygen down into it and forms D.O. The third and most complicated process that produces dissolved oxygen is photosynthesis. This is the process by which green plants change sunlight energy into food energy. Here's how it works: aquatic plants take in carbon dioxide and water. In the presence of sunlight and chlorophyll (the chemical which makes plants green), the plant turns those materials into sugar and leftover oxygen. This "waste" oxygen is then released into the stream and becomes dissolved oxygen for the animals to use.

Unfortunately, there may not always be enough dissolved oxygen in a stream. Why? One reason may be because the water is warm. Warm liquids cannot hold as much gas. You know what happens when you open a warm soda!

Next year you will have to measure D.O. in streams, so you should learn as much as you can about D.O. and how it effects the stream and its critters.

AND NOW SOME MORE WORDS FROM LAST YEAR'S WATERSHED CLASS:

Congratulations!! You have the once in a lifetime chance to be in Watershed. You should treasure the next year; you may never experience it again. —Chad M.

You are going to have a great year. Enjoy it while you can. —Sarah A.

Don't fool around! When you get a big project to do, don't just wait until the last minute. Plan your time wisely. —Eric A.

This year has been so short. When we talk about getting out in a few weeks, I think back, and it seems like we just started. It's fair to warn you: don't waste a moment of your time, because you never get it back. Enjoy it while you have it. It was the best school year I've had.   —Matt O.

Being in Watershed is an opportunity that ends once the year does. So take the chance that you get, because you won't get another one. —Lauren B.

This is probably the best time in your life to learn. I think I have learned more than I ever have before. I think I will always remember the things that I have done in this class. —Greg C.

Things you have to know about being in Watershed:
— always complete assignments and turn them in on time
— always give 100% if not more
— use your time wisely
— abide by the five C's
— always do your share of the work and give your share of ideas if you are working in a group. —Kelly M.

Your upcoming Watershed year will probably be your best school year ever. You will have a lot of fun discovering the life in our streams, and at the same time you will learn. At first I wasn't certain about what to expect when I first came here, but now that my Watershed year is coming to an end, I don't want to leave. —Cynthia G.

This year you are going to have the time of your life, and you're also going to have a lot of work. You need to learn how to manage your time. —Maggie M.

Hope you enjoy your year in Watershed as much as I did. —Mike H.

Writing this letter, I'm both happy and sad. I'm happy for you because you are going to have an excellent year in Watershed. I am sad because writing this letter means that I am nearing the end of my Watershed year, and this I am not looking forward to. Make good use of your time, and have a great year as a Watersheder. —Sarah T.

Probably the best advice I could give you is don't let the year slip by. You have nine months of Watershed, but it seems like one. Put every moment of your year to good use.
—Ben T.

Mr. Silcox and Mr. Springer will always want you to hand in quality work! Time + Creativity + Work + Thinking = Quality work. They always want the best of you.
—Amir Z.

First of all, you will have to get over your fear of bugs; I mean, if you have one. Then on the days that you have trips to the streams, make sure you bring a change of clothes. Who knows when you will slip off a rock and plunge into the creek! —Geoff S.

The more you put into Watershed, the more you get out of Watershed. If you are the type of person who will do more than what's required, you will have more fun. The more you do, the more fun you'll have. —Bryan K.

First of all, you become practically best friends with everyone in your Watershed group. The second thing that Watershed does for you is teach you to get organized. But above all the others, you learn about all the things around you. What I'm trying to say in all of this is that Watershed was the best year of my life; and, believe me, I'm not just saying this, I truly mean it. —Bobby M.

There is a lot of work to do. Don't think you can just do it later. Spread your work out, and practice your responsibilities and your organizational skills. —Dan M.

You will be totally soaked on about 30 occasions . . . but you'll learn a great deal. We have a very good reputation with many people and organizations. Please keep that reputation for more Watershed classes to come. — Jordan N.

In the beginning of the year you have the same amount of work you have in "school," but as the year progresses you get more and more. Trust me, your hands will be filled with work! But when you're finished, you can have a lot of fun with your spare time. Watershed is a lot of fun, but use your time wisely: get your work in, then play. Watershed is a lot better than school. — Kyle S.-E.

I hope you have fun. I know I did! —Rebecca G.

I have only one piece of advice; that is, do everything quickly, and early, because you're going to find it gets harder and harder to hand things in on time. —David C.

The main lesson for you to learn in Watershed is to plan your time well. Stop and think about it once in awhile: are you accomplishing your goals? —Leily L.

Some people think Watershed is a place to fool around; but even though you don't get grades, you still have a commitment! —Tracy K.

In Watershed you really learn things that you will find interesting and fun. Even those things like history that are sometimes boring to learn are taught in really cool ways, like actually visiting the battle sites . . . — Sarah B.

Next year you guys are getting, I think, the best opportunity of your life. In Watershed you will learn to do things as a group, as well as individually. No matter what, you will do a lot of writing! But the thing to remember is to have fun! —Becky L.

APPENDIX C
Structured Reports

The following section presents the instructions used for the ten structured research reports used in the first year of the program. As the program changed over the years, most these reports have remained, though sometimes in altered forms or with added criteria. Nevertheless, these will give the reader a sense of the scope and the structure of that first year. The "Reports Overview" provided was written for the formal pilot evaluation; hence the references to subject area emphases.

WATERSHED REPORTS OVERVIEW

No.	Title	Area	Format	Map	Illust.	Bibliography (Minimums)
1	PLANTS	Science	Phrase Outline	No	Yes	2 sources
2	ANIMALS	Science	Sentence Outline	No	Yes	3 sources
3	GEOLOGIC SCIENCE TOPIC	Science	Outline / Paragraphs	Yes	No	3 sources
4	ADOPT-A GUEST	Varied	Letter / Report	No	No	No
5	HISTORY TOPIC	History	Report	Yes	Yes	4 sources
6	TOWN-SHIPS	History / Science	Letter / Interview / Report	Yes	Yes	Various
7	YEAR IN REVIEW	History	Newspaper Articles	Yes	Yes	No
8	ENVIRON-MENTAL ISSUES	Science / Social Studies	Report	Optional		5 sources
9	BRANDY-WINE BIOGRAPHY	Various	Outline / Report	Optional		4 sources
10	STATE OF BRANDYWINE VALLEY	All Areas	Essays / Report	Yes	Yes	Various
	SELF-EVALUATION	Affective	Short Essays	No	No	No

WATERSHED

**Report #1: Plants
(Phrase Outline)**

NAME:_____   DATE:_____

Directions: Use at least two books to research the following plant subject for the
types of information listed. Keep an accurate record of your sources.
On a separate sheet of paper, write your phrase outline using the pattern shown here. Draw a picture of your subject. Attach your outline
and your picture to this sheet and turn it in, along with your bibliography, by _____.

TOPIC: _____

I.   Classification
    A. Genus / species
    B. Family
    C. Order
    D. Class
    E. Phylum
    F. Kingdom

II. Physical description
    A. Size / Shape
    B. Color
    C. Distinctive characteristics

III. Habitat
    A. Where it is found
    B. Place on the food chain

IV. Additional interesting characteristics / information

WATERSHED

Report #2: Animals

(Sentence Outline)

NAME:_____   DATE:_____

Directions: Use at least three books to research the following animal subject for the
types of information listed. Keep an accurate record of your sources.
On a separate sheet, write your sentence outline using the pattern
shown here. Draw a picture of your subject. Attach your outline and
your picture to this sheet and turn it in, along with your bibliography
by _____.

TOPIC:_____

I.   Classification
        A. Genus / species
        B. Family
        C. Order
        D. Class
        E. Phylum
        F. Kingdom

II. Physical description
        A. Size / Shape
        B. Color
        C. Distinctive features

III. Habitat
        A. Where it lives
        B. Place on the food chain

IV. Additional interesting characteristics / information

WATERSHED

Report #3: Geo-science

(Paragraphs)

NAME:_____   DATE:_____

Directions: Research the following geo-science topic for the types of information
          listed. Write a phrase outline using the three-part pattern shown at
          the bottom of this page.

Your outline is due on _____.

Once your outline has been approved, transcribe it into a report consisting of three
paragraphs—a paragraph for each of the Roman numeral sections of your outline.

In addition, draw a map of the Brandywine valley and show where your topic is located.
You must also turn in a bibliography of at least three sources. (As always, encyclopedia
do not count ! !)

Your final report, map and bibliography are due by _____

TOPIC:_____

Outlin /paragraph pattern:

I.   Topic description/definition: physical details

II. Topic location: where it is found

III. Topic significance: how it is important to the Brandywine valley

WATERSHED

Report #4: Adopt-A-Guest

(Introduction/Letter)

NAME:_____   DATE:_____

Directions: Research _____. Find out as much as you can about
                  his or her background, occupation, and significance in the Brandywine
                  valley. As part of your research, you must write a letter to this person.
                  This letter must include:

                  1.   a brief introduction describing our program and your project

                  2.   specific questions to help you get information about the person

                  3.   an invitation asking your person if he / she would be willing to
                       come speak to the class.

You must then write a short biographical report about your person based on your research. This report should be suitable as an introduction for your person if he / she can
come to the class. Whether your guest can come or not, you will present your report to
the class.

A rough copy of the letter is due by _____.

The final copy is due by _____.
(Reports will be scheduled according to your guest's response.)

ADDRESS: _____

                      _____

WATERSHED

Report #5: Historical Topic

(Full Report Format)

NAME:_____   DATE:_____

Directions: Use at least four sources to find as much information as you can concerning the topic listed below. As always, keep an accurate record of your sources. Try to find information explaining

— what the topic was / is
— where it was / is
— when it was / is
— why it was / is important to the watershed

Submit a phrase outline of your report by _____

Once your phrase outline has been approved, write out your report in expository paragraphs. Draw an illustration of your topic and a map showing its location(s) within the watershed. The final report, illustration, map and bibliography are due by

_____.

TOPIC:_____

WATERSHED

Report #6: Chester County Townships

NAME:_____   DATE:_____

PARTNER:_____

TOWNSHIP:_____

Directions: You and your partner are responsible throughout this year for finding out as much as you can about the township listed. This paper sets out certain guidelines and due dates for you to follow. keep this paper in your folder at all times, and have us initial it as you complete each section.

Teacher / Date

I.   Find out the name and address of an (elected) official of the township by _____.

Name:_____

Address:_____

_____   _____

II. Write a rough draft of a letter to that official by _____.   _____

Checklist: A. Introduce yourself and Watershed.
              B. Explain that you are gathering data for a report.
              C. Ask the person to describe:
                  1. Why is your township important to the Brandywine valley?
                  2. How is it unique?
              D. Emphasize that we are interested in issues such as:
                  1. the history
                  2. the river's impact on the area
                  3. the area's impact on the river
                  4. what the people/gov't do about:
                      a. parks and open space
                      b. zoning regulations
                      c. anti-pollution laws
                      d. health and human services
                  5. industry and agriculture in the area
                  6. plans for the future.

Teacher / Date

III.   Write and mail a good copy of the letter on RMS stationery by _____.   _____

IV.   Draw a detailed / scale map of the township by _____.   _____

V.   Research and write a brief history of the area by _____.   _____

Checklist: A. Who, when and why first settled
                 B. Important people, events, etc.
                 C. Growth and development, major industries, etc.

VI.   Answer to your letter received: _____   _____

VII.   Prepare a follow-up interview to expand on the answers received. (Due date to be determined by date response is received.)   _____

VIII.   Conduct the interview (by phone or in person).   _____

IX.   Create at least 3 drawings or 12 photographs of your topic by _____.   _____

X.   Interpret and summarize the results of your letter and interview by _____.   _____

XI.   Present all your materials, including bibliography, in a booklet with a cover. All text is to be set up and printed on a computer / word processor. Due by_____.   _____

XII.   Make an oral presentation to the class on a date to be scheduled after all else is completed. Date:_____.   _____

XIII.   Write a one page evaluation of your own work. Discuss problems you encountered and successes you achieved. Due by_____.   _____

WATERSHED

Report #7: A Year In Review

(Newspaper)

NAME:_____   DATE:_____

Directions: Research the year _____. Then create a newspaper that reviews the events and the "atmosphere" of that year. Your paper must include the following sections:

— World News
— American / Local News
— Births and Obituaries
— Editorials
— Comics

In addition, your paper must include at least three (3) of the following optional sections:

— Fashions
— Food
— Advice Columns (e.g. "Dear Abby")
— Want Ads / Personals
— Travel / Transportation
— Architecture / Real Estate
— Science News
— Culture / Entertainment
— Letters to the Editor

Remember: Each section should consist of no less than four (4) articles; and news articles, though concise. should answer the questions: *Who, What, Where, When, How* and *Why*. Also, don't forget an original title! !

Your Newspaper is due by _____

NOTE: This project was subsequently expanded to a three-year period with slightly more specific instructions. For example, maps and illustrations were later required, as were specific numbers of articles in the world and local news sections.

WATERSHED

Report #8: Environmental Issues

(Report Format w/Annotated Bibliography)

NAME:_____   DATE:_____

TOPIC:_____

Directions: This will be both a written and an oral report designed to help you learn about important environmental issues and how they effect the Brandywine valley. You are to research as fully as you can the topic-issue listed. Keep careful records of your sources, and construct a preliminary outline before writing your final report.

Your written report must convey the following information:

1. a definition of your topic-issue
2. an explanation of why the problem exists and what causes it
3. an explanation of how the problem is measured
4. a detailed description of how the topic effects living organisms
5. a description of how the problem specifically effects the Brandywine valley
6. an evaluation of how the issue/problem is increasing or decreasing world-wide, nationally, and locally
7. specific recommendations for alleviating (lessening) or eliminating (solving) the problem.

Along with your written report, you must turn in an annotated bibliography*. It must include at least one (1) entry from each of the following categories:

- magazines
- newspapers
- reference books
- primary source books
- audio/visual sources

Your written report and annotated bibliography are due by_____.
(A time for your oral report will be scheduled after your written report has been approved.)

* Annotated bibliography means that each of your entries must be accompanied by a short description of its specific contents.

WATERSHED

Report #9: Brandywine Valley Biography

(Outline/Report Format)

NAME:_____   DATE:_____

SUBJECT:_____

Directions: You are to find out as much as you can about your subject, a person who played an important role in the Brandywine valley. Your report will be turned in first in outline form and must include:

    I.   Biographical data: when and where the person was born, lived and died.

    II. Childhood: a brief and general description of the person's family background, childhood and education.

    III. Contribution: a detailed description of the person's adult life, with particular emphasis on the accomplishments which made him or her important.

    IV. Evaluation: your assessment of the person's impact (effect) on the Brandywine valley.

Once your outline is approved, you will transcribe the report into narrative form.

You must also turn in a bibliography that contains at least four entries, not including encyclopedia.

Your written outline and bibliography are due on _____.

After your outline has been approved, you will be assigned a date and time to present your final written report orally to the class.

WATERSHED

Report #10: The State of the Brandywine

NAME:_____   DATE:_____

Report Ten is your opportunity to "show-off" what you have learned in WATERSHED this year. This is not a research report, though you may certainly do additional research if you wish. Instead, it is to be a summary of all the information you have gathered throughout this year.

Your report is to include all six sections listed below, with each section separately numbered and titled. The general description or summary portion of each of the first four sections is to be followed by a detailed description of a topic/subject that you believe best illustrates that section.

I.   Geographic description of the valley

II.   Description of the valley's natural history

III.   Summary of the valley's historical development

IV.   Description of the current condition of the valley

V.   Description of the valley's future

VI.   A map showing aspects from each of the other areas.

Remember: This is to be your best work!   Someone who knows nothing of the Brandywine should be able to read your report and learn.

APPENDIX D

Sample Folder Comment Sheets

The following section surveys the various weekly folder sheets used in WATER-SHED over the years. For most years, the folder consisted of two sheets: one for a record of assignments, and one for evaluative comments. They are presented here in chronological order. The reader should realize that none of these has proven totally satisfactory: further refinements will undoubtedly ensue.

WATERSHED WEEKLY COMMENT SHEET   (1987- 89)

NAME:_____

DATE	TEACHER COMMENT	PARENT COMMENT / INITIAL

WHEN THIS SHEET IS FILLED IN, TURN IT IN AND GET A NEW ONE FOR YOUR FOLDER.

WATERSHED: STUDENT'S ASSIGNMENT SHEET   (1987 - 90)

NAME:_____

| DATE | ASSIGNMENT | DUE DATE | CONFIRMATIONS | |
			TEACHER	PARENT

WATERSHED: WEEKLY FOLDER PROGRESS REVIEW   (1990- 92)

NAME:_____

DATE	STUDENT'S COMMENTS	PARENT RESPONSE / SIGNATURE

WATERSHED: DAILY ACCOMPLISHMENT RECORD   (1991 - 92)

NAME:_____

FROM: THURSDAY_____ TO WEDNESDAY_____

DAY   DATE   ACCOMPLISHMENTS

THURSDAY

FRIDAY

WATERSHED WEEKLY FOLDER SHEET   (1992 - 93)

NAME:_____

THURSDAY:_____Question:_____

Assignments due Today:_____
Math:_____
Future Assignments:_____

Accomplishments:

FRIDAY:_____Question:_____

WATERSHED: WEEKLY PROGRESS REVIEW SHEET   (1992 - 94)

Name:_____

Date: _____

Student's Comment:_____

_____

_____

_____

_____

_____

_____

_____

_____

Student's Goal:_____

Teacher's Comments

_____

_____

_____

_____

_____

_____

_____

_____

Parent Comments

_____

_____

_____

_____

_____

WATERSHED   DAILY LOG SHEET   (1993 - 94)

NAME:_____

THURSDAY:_____Question:_____

_____

_____

_____

_____

_____

_____

_____

Accomplishments:

FRIDAY:_____Question:_____

_____

_____

_____

_____

_____

The following section is a copy of the application packet originally implemented for Year Five (1991 - 92). The essays were subsequently removed from the packet in Year Six as is explained in Chapter 8.   I have also included a copy of the acceptance confirmation that the parents turn in after the required informational meeting.

SO, YOU WANT TO BE IN WATERSHED?

READ THIS

WATERSHED: A WHOLE LEARNING ALTERNATIVE

Program Description

WATERSHED is an alternative to the traditional middle school curriculum. Approximately thirty-six students elect to spend their seventh grade year—all day, every day—examining specific watersheds. These students learn skills and concepts through an interdisciplinary combination of classroom and on-site learning experiences. Elements and processes from language arts, science, social studies, the arts, and physical education are included. Only two courses are taken outside the WATERSHED program. Students are enrolled in the regular foreign language class of their choosing, and they work with a math teacher to supplement appropriate math experiences which are integrated into the program.

The WATERSHED program de-emphasizes traditional classroom procedures such as lectures and teacher-directed activities. Individual research, small group projects, and first-hand exploratory experiences with teacher guidance are emphasized. This places a great deal of responsibility on the student as he / she is required to decide how portions of each day will be spent.

Beyond the classroom, WATERSHED students take trips to museums, historic sites, and other places important to the watershed. Students also participate in field study trips to the streams to measure portions of the river; to take chemical, physical, and biotic measurements; and to observe and describe plants and animals. Students record their results and experiences in writing, art, and film.

The WATERSHED program is non-graded. Communications concerning the students' performance go home weekly in the form of an assignment / comment folder which each student maintains throughout the year. Again, the emphasis is on fostering the students' self-motivation, self-discipline and self-esteem. Success in WATERSHED is measured by the individual student's willingness to exceed minimal requirements. All the activities are designed to promote this commitment, along with caring, courage, caution, and cooperation.

The cooperative spirit also extends to the parents who are directly involved in the students' learning. Parents often accompany the class on trips, visit the classroom regularly, review the students' work weekly, and communicate frequently with the teachers. Throughout their tenure and beyond the parents help evaluate and amend the program.

WATERSHED is at once a unique opportunity and a serious responsibility for each student who undertakes it. As in all things, the more effort each student puts into WATERSHED, the more all benefit from it. Please read the list of participant responsibilities on the next page, and think carefully about your willingness to do your very best.

WATERSHED: PARTICIPANTS' RESPONSIBILITIES

I. STUDENTS: Each student who elects to participate in the WATERSHED program will be expected

generally:

    a to produce quality work that is complete and on time

    b. to look for wider relationships and applications

    c. to take an active and positive part in all our activities

    d. to take pride in his / her work and progress

    e to accept responsibility for his / her behavior and accomplishments

    f. to go beyond basic, stated expectations;

specifically:

    a. to pay attention and cooperate at all times

    b. to keep a daily, written log summarizing his / her day's activities and setting goals for the following day

    c. to take home and share with his / her parents the weekly assignment folder

    d. to complete a minimum of 1/2 hour of WATERSHED related reading, writing or research each evening

    e. to take proper care of the materials and equipment provided

    f. to try new experiences with a positive attitiude, eg., handling aquatic organisms

    g. to withstand with a positive attitude the physical discomforts that may accompany long bus rides, being wet for extended periods, and being outdoors in all types of weather

    h. to be concerned for safety in all situations.

In short, we expect each student to act in accordance with the **"FIVE C's"** of

Commitment   **Cooperation**   **Courage**   **Caring**   **Caution**

II.   PARENTS who elect to participate in the WATERSHED program will be expected:

a.   to show an active interest in their student's learning experiences

b.   to support their student's progress toward fulfilling his / her responsibilities as listed above

c.   to reinforce the student's efforts by

- discussing each day's activities with the child

- following the progress of specific assignments

- checking and signing the weekly folder

- insisting that the student devote at least 1/2 hour per evening to WATER-SHED-related homework

d.   to become directly involved in WATERSHED activities whenever possible, eg., Open Houses, meetings, field trips

e.   to communicate questions and concerns to the teachers whenever the need arises.

WATERSHED: PRELIMINARY APPLICATION   NAME:_____

If you would like to be considered eligible to become a WATERSHED participant for next year, you MUST complete BOTH SIDES of this form and reyturn it to the Middle School office by May _____.

A final list of eligible students will be determined by a totally random selection taken from the students who complete and turn in this form. After attending a required question and answer session, parents will then be asked to make a final decision regarding their child's actual participation in WATERSHED.

On the back of this page, please answer the following questions to the best of your ability:

1. What do you hope to gain from the WATERSHED experience?

2. Why do you think you would make a good member of next year's WATERSHED group?

I have read and I understand the program description and the participants' responsibilities.

STUDENT SIGNATURE:_____

PARENT SIGNATURE:_____

I want to be a member of next year's WATERSHED, and I promise that I will do my best to fulfill the responsibilities of a WATERSHED participant.

STUDENT SIGNATURE:_____

I would like my child's name placed on the list for random selection to the WATERSHED program for next year.

PARENT SIGNATURE:_____

WATERSHED   ACCEPTANCE CONFIRMATION

Student's Name:_____

Participant # _____

Alternate # _____

Please check the appropriate space below and then return this form to the Middle School Office by this Friday, May _____.

_____   Yes, we want to participate in the WATERSHED program.

_____   No, we have decided NOT to participate in the WATERSHED program.
            Please allow the next person on the list to take our place.

Student Signature:_____

Parent Signature:_____

Those participants who accept a place in the WATERSHED program for next year will be receiving in June a packet of information and summer assignments. At that time, we will also get together for a group photograph of next year's participants.

In the meantime, if you have any questions, please do not hesitate to drop by the WATERSHED room or contact us at 688 - 8100 ext. 271.

Learning Station Overviews

Appendix F contains the Learning Station overviews and samples of some of the station descriptions which we used in Year Five (1991-92). These are copies of the papers that the students received to help them structure their work. Though we abandoned the learning station format, per se, after that year, the concepts and many of the activities included in them remain part of the program.

LEARNING STATIONS OVERVIEW

The WATERSHED room, along with other features, includes six learning station areas. Two of these stations will remain constant throughout the year, Microscopy and Photography; the other four will change totally with each new program emphasis (that is Sense of Place, Sense of Time, and Sense of Quality).

PURPOSE: The purpose of these Learning Stations is to provide the students with
— the means to discover a common body of information and skills
— the opportunity to learn at their own pace and according to their own interests and needs.

STRUCTURE: Each Learning Station contains:
— an OVERVIEW SHEET which lists
  • the purpose of the station
  • specific learning responsibilities
  • required activities and projects
  • optional or recommended activities
— a box of 3 x 5 cards which detail the activities and ask significant guide questions. (Green = required activities, Blue = recommended activities.)
— many of the materials and resources needed to complete the activities on the cards.

PROCEDURE:
1. Begin by familiarizing yourself with the Overview of each station. What are you trying to learn at each station? What activities are required?
2. Set aside a section of your research notebook for each Learning Station.
3. In the class time provided or as homework, select and complete as many activities as you can. Keep all your results together in the appropriate section of your notebook or binder. Always record the card number and the question or activity. REMEMBER: Blue cards give you added information or skills to help you complete the Green cards. The more Blue cards you complete, the more you will be prepared for the review seminars.
4. Turn in Green card assignments as you complete them. Blue card activities are not handed in, but you must bring them to the review seminars.

BOTTOM LINE(S): There is a DIRECT RELATIONSHIP between learning and effort. You get out according to what you put in! The choice is yours. When in doubt, ASK!!

SENSE OF PLACE: OBJECTIVES

From now until November, our emphasis in WATERSHED is on the sense of PLACE: that is, helping you develop an understanding of WHERE you are.

During the first week of November, you and one or two of your classmates will participate in a seminar discussion with two of the teachers. In this seminar, you will be expected to demonstrate what you have learned in response to the following questions:

1. What is a watershed?

2. Why are watersheds important?

3. Where are the Gulph and Darby Creek watersheds located?

4. In what ways are the two watersheds similar and different?

Your objective, your goal between now and the first week in November is to learn as much as you can to help answer these questions as completely as possible. Everything we do over the next ten weeks should help you develop your answers to these major questions. We will be reading informative articles together and giving you helpful log questions daily. We will be asking you to write specific reports and essays each week to help you pull together information. We will be taking trips through the watersheds and seeing first-hand many of the organisms, processes and features we are asking you to know.

LEARNING STATIONS

To aid you more, six interrelated learning stations have been set up. Each station is designed to provide you with activities which will lead you to important information you will need. The six stations are: Cartography, Geology, Processes, Ecology, Photography, and Microscopy.

Each station has required activities (on GREEN cards) and optional activities (on BLUE cards). The optional activities are included to help you understand and complete the required activities, which in turn help you answer the major seminar questions. The order in which you complete activities is up to you, as is the number of optional activities you decide to complete. (Obviously, the more you do, the better you will be able to answer the seminar questions !) You will be keeping a record of and notes on each station and the activities you complete. You will be able to use these notes in the seminar discussions.

We are here to assist you; so are your classmates. If you have questions, ASK !!

SENSE OF PLACE: LEARNING STATION—CARTOGRAPHY

Goals: To learn the physical features of the watersheds we are studying.
To learn map reading and map making skills.

Specifics: You MUST be able to describe the following physical features of
the watersheds:

— the location of the headwaters and of the mouth
— the length of each stream
— the direction of the flow
— the gradient
— the drainage area
— the average velocity and flow
— the tributaries
— the general topography and geomorphic features
— land use patterns and population areas.

Required Activities:
(Green Cards)

— Construct a 3-dimensional topographic map of the Gulph Creek
watershed
— Create a Gradient Profile for each stream
— Write a short essay or script which describes how the physical
features of the watersheds are similar and different.

Recommended Activities:
(Blue Cards)

— Map Vocabulary (1)	— Map Reading (13)
— Geomorphology Vocabulary (1)	— Geomorphology (2)
— Gradient (2)	— Drainage Area (1)
— Compass Skills (4)	— Climate / Weather (4)
— Population (3)	

SENSE OF PLACE: LEARNING STATION—GEOLOGY

Goals: To recognize the local rocks.
To describe how they were formed.
To name the minerals which make them up.
To locate where that can be found locally.
To explain how they influence topography and land use.

Required Activities:
(Green Cards)

— Draw a map of the region showing underlying geologic structure
— Make a diagram of the rock cycle
— Make a chart showing geologic time
— Describe the "Fall Line"

Recommended Activities:
(Blue Cards)

— Rock / Mineral (1)
— Rock Types (1)
— Limestone (7)
— Schist (3)
— Gneiss (3)
— Serpentinite (4)
— Quartzite (4)
— Coastal Plain (1)

SENSE OF PLACE: LEARNING STATION— PROCESSES

Goals: To describe how the basic elements for life cycle through our environment.
To list the main processes in the water cycle.
To explain the processes of Photosynthesis and Respiration.
To describe a local food chain.

Required Activities:
(Green Cards)

> — Water cycle interpretation
> — Importance of photosynthesis essay
> — Draw the "circle" of Photosynthesis and Respiration
> — Construct a local stream food chain
> — The adventures of "C"
> — List at least four ways nitrogen is important to you
> — Why is Mr. Silcox 4.5 billion years old
> — Rock cycle diagram

Recommended Activities:
(Blue Cards)

> — Water cycle (4)
> — Photosynthesis (4)
> — Respiration (5)
> — Food chains (5)
> — Chemical cycles (1)
> — Carbon-oxygen cycle (2)
> — Nitrogen cycle (1)
> — Phosphorus (2)

SENSE OF PLACE: LEARNING STATION—ECOLOGY

Goals: To recognize some of the important plants and animals which inhabit our streams
To understand how they live.
To examine the relationships between them and their total environment.

Required Activities:
(Green Cards)

— Draw from life: mayfly, caddisfly, crayfish
  Duckweed, milfoil, elodea
— Draw a stream "Food Web"
— Select one of the animals and describe its adaptations to stream life
— Select one of the plants and describe its adaptations to stream life.
— Describe the differences in plants and animals as stream order
  increases.

Recommended Activities:
(Blue Cards)

— Mayfly
— Dragonfly
— Caddisfly
— Planaria
— Crayfish
— Elodea
— Duckweed
— Milfoil
— Filamentous algae

SENSE OF TIME: OBJECTIVES

From now until early next March, our emphasis in WATERSHED will be on the sense of TIME: that is, helping you develop an understanding of when and how your life fits into the chronology of this area.

During the first week in March, you and one or two of your classmates will participate in a seminar discussion with your two teachers. In this seminar, you will be expected to demonstrate what you have learned in response to the following questions:

1. Who has lived in this region at different times?

2. What was it like to live in this area at different times?

3. How have different peoples changed (and been changed by) the area?

4. What role have the streams played in the course of history?

Your objective, your goal between now and the first week of March is to learn as much as you can to help answer these general questions as completely as possible. Everything we do as a class during this period should help you develop your answers to these major questions. We will read some materials together, and we will continue to give you daily log questions pertaining to the sense of Time. We will take trips to museums and historic sites in the watersheds, and we will ask you to work on at least two special projects and several essays.

In addition, you will again have six learning stations to complete:

The Leni-Lenape	New Sweden	The Quaker Colony
The Revolutionary War	Photography	Microscopy

Each station has required activities on GREEN cards and recommended activities on BLUE cards. While we will be following a chronological order in our class work, discussions and special projects; you may work on these learning stations in any order you wish. Be sure to keep track of the activities you complete. As always, the more you do, the more you will learn and understand about the Sense of Time.

If you have questions, ASK! !

SENSE OF TIME: LEARNING STATION—LENI-LENAPE

Purpose: This station is designed to give you an understanding of what life was like in this region before the arrival of the first European settlers.

When you finish this station, you should be able to answer the following general questions:
— Who were the Leni-Lenape?
— Where did they live?
— What was their life-style like?
— How did they view this land?
— What happened to the Lenape after the Europeans arrived?
— What contributions did the Lenape make to our culture?

Required Activities:
(Green Cards)

1. Draw a map of this region and locate on it Lenape trails and towns.
2. Research and then make an "authentic" Lenape implement, piece of clothing or adornment, or a model of a Lenape canoe, wigwam, or village.
3. AMERICAN DIARY #1: You are a Lenape living along the banks of Darby Creek in the year 1640. Describe a day in your life. Include information revealing how you feel about "the land between two trees," and how you feel about the Swedes or Dutch you have recently met.
4. Be prepared to answer all the questions on the handout sheet.

Recommended Activities:
(Blue Cards)

— Vocabulary terms
— Locate modern place-names based on Lenape words
— Make a poster depicting some aspect of life in a Lenape village
— Write a script for a play or a video documentary about Lenape life
— Create a board game which would teach others about Lenape life
— Make a poster of a deer and show how Lenape used the various parts
— Try to write a poem using Lenape words
— Make a poster or annotated map describing Lenape seasonal migration
— Draw a picture showing how Lenape dressed
— Prepare a Lenape meal
— Write a script to enact the Lenape creation myth
— Make a map of northeastern America and show the location of other Native American groups
— Develop an idea of your own to show your knowledge of Lenape life.

SENSE OF TIME: LEARNING STATION —NEW SWEDEN

Purpose: This station is designed to give you an understanding of the first European colonization of this region.

When you finish this station, you should be able to answer the following general questions:

— When, where and why did the Swedes establish a colony in this area?
— What problems did these early colonists face?
— What was life like in the colony, and how did it compare with life in Sweden and in Europe in general?
— What happened to the colony?
— What contributions did this early Swedish colony make to our culture?

Required Activities:
(Green Cards)

1. Draw a map of this region and locate on it Swedish settlements.
2. Draw a picture of the Kalmar Nyckel.
3. Write a dialogue between two or more Swedish settlers in the year 1650. At least one speaker should represent the original settlers from 1638, the other (s) should be newer arrivals. Their conversation should illustrate what life was like in the colony.
4. Be prepared to answer all of the specific questions on the handout sheet.

Recommended Activities:
(Blue Cards)

— Vocabulary terms
— Locate modern place-names based on Swedish words or names
— Draw a picture or make a model of a Swedish fort
— Draw a picture or make a model of a Swedish log cabin
— Draw a picture or make a model of a Swedish mill
— Select a well-known person of Swedish heritage and describe his / her contribution to America or the world.
— Prepare a Swedish meal
— Describe a Swedish festival or holiday ritual and, if possible, compare it to its American counterpart
— Research and present a biography of one of the important historical figures mentioned in your reading packet
— Develop an idea of your own to illustrate your knowledge of life in New Sweden.

SENSE OF TIME: LEARNING STATION— PHOTOGRAPHY

Goals: To recognize the elements of composition
To shoot a well composed, well exposed photograph
To develop a roll of black and white film
To print black and white photographs

Required Activities:
(Green Cards)

1.   Carefully select a portrait in one of our books.
— describe how the photographer reveals the subject
— what does the portrait tell you about the subject?
— describe how the photographer used the following
elements of composition to create the portrait:
— lighting
— depth of field
— focal length
— contrast
— balance
— line
— the rule of thirds
— background
— props
— special effects

2.   Develop a roll of Tri-X film (Black and White, ISO 400)
—memorize all procedural steps and times
—practice required techniques (opening film canister, spooling
film, etc.) before going into the darkroom

3.   Print a black and white photograph
-—memorize all procedural steps and times

Recommended Activities:
(Blue Cards)

Select photographs from our books which you consider to be effective. Note the
techniques the photographers used to create these images.

SENSE OF TIME: LEARNING STATION—MICROSCOPY

Goal: To continue to use the microscope as a tool to examine a variety of objects.

Required Activities:
(Green Cards)

1. Pick one or more of the prepared slides from the "monthly selection" box.
    —Set up the Monocular Microscope with your slide on the stage.
    —Draw the object at both low and high power.
    (REMEMBER: ALWAYS FOCUS UP !)
    —Include title, magnification, your name, and a brief description of the object on your drawing.

2. Select a natural object (e.g., rock, leaf, benthic invertebrate) to examine with the Binocular Microscope.
    —Draw the object at both 15 and 30 power.
    —Include title, magnification, your name, and a brief description of the object on your drawing.

3. Place several drops of water from our culture dishes onto a reservoir slide.
    —On <u>low power only</u> search the slide for interesting objects and then draw what you see.
    —Include title, magnification, your name, and a brief description of the object on your drawing.

Recommended Activities:
(Blue Cards)

—   Examine the other prepared slides.
—   Conduct a "Protozoan Search" with the Monocular Microscope, a reservoir slide and the cultures.

SENSE OF QUALITY: OBJECTIVES

From now until the end of our WATERSHED year, our emphasis will be on the sense of QUALITY: that is, an evaluation of the systems that effect the quality of your life in this region.

To accomplish this we will be examining the parallel systems in three "organisms:" the human body, the homes in which we live, and the region as a whole. We will examine each in terms of its form and its function, and we will look for similarities and differences among the three.

By the final review seminar in June, you should be able to describe the forms and functions of each, as well as their similarities and differences. You should know how each gets, distributes and maintains energy resources; how each handles the waste products it creates; what problems each faces and how each confronts those problems to ensure its survival and improvement. Ultimately, you should be able to describe how each effects the Quality of YOUR life now and in the future.

To help you understand these complex relationships, we have devised three projects in lieu of the green cards from Place and Time.

For the Human Body you will each complete nine worksheets on the body systems. Then you will write an essay / story detailing an epic journey through the body.

For the House, you will work in pairs to design a viable house for a particular location. You will also build a scale model from your floor plans and elevations.

Finally, in groups of three or four, you will redesign the Darby Creek watershed for the year 2020.

Instead of blue cards for these projects, we will be presenting you with specific tasks that must be completed before you can successfully fulfill the requirements of the larger project.

In addition, Microscopy and Photography learning station requirements have been made part of these three larger projects. Details for all of these activities will be presented as the need arises.

As always, if you have questions,   ASK! !

SENSE OF QUALITY: PROJECT—HUMAN BODY

Mission: As head of the most respected medical team in the United States, you are chosen to locate and cure a dangerous disorder affecting one of the world's most important people.

In order to do this, you must be reduced to the size of a glucose molecule and injected into the patient's body.

Describe your travels as you search for the source of the disorder, locate it and work to cure it.

Preparation:

1. Select a disease / dysfunction and write it down.
2. Decide which systems you will include in your journey (at least <u>five</u>, as many as nine); make a list.
3. Decide which organs you will include in your journey (more than <u>ten</u>) and make a list.
4. Outline the plot of your "Fantastic Voyage," listing the important stages of the journey (systems / organs) in order.
5. Include in your outline important plot elements as well as active verbs and adjectives you will be using.

Procedure:

You must: <u>Describe</u>   the disorder
your journey to the source of the disorder
how you locate the disorder
how you work to cure the disorder
your journey back out of the patient

* * * Include at least five systems and more than ten organs * * *

Timeline: Criteria Due _____
Outline Due _____
Essay Due _____

SENSE OF QUALITY: PROJECT—HOUSE DESIGN

You and a partner are to design a house for a family of four with a family income of about $75,000 per year. The house is to be "built" on a plot of land no greater that one (1) acre in size. You may choose where it will be located, but you will be asked to account for climate and land conditions.

The final project will include:

— a "preconstruction" plot description and diagram to show size, shape, topographic features, compass bearings and climatic conditions

— a "post-construction" landscaping diagram to show how you fit the house into its environment

— floor plans including basic heating / cooling and electrical considerations

— basic plumbing plans (overlays work best here)

— a frontal elevation

— a model built to a scale of 1/4 inch = 1 foot

— a brief summary of the house's special features

Drawn aspects due by _____

Model due by _____

SENSE OF QUALITY: PROJECT—REGIONAL PLAN

As part of our look at the quality of life in our watersheds, we ask you to form a group of three of four to think about the future.

Start by drawing a good base map of Darby Creek Watershed which shows the streams and the major topographical features. This map should be transferred to poster board once it is approved.

Now imagine that the year is 2020. You and the others in your group are adults, and you are members of the regional planning commission for the Darby Creek Watershed. The area in 2020 has a population of between 250,000 and 300,000 people.

You are to create three (3) overlay maps on acetate which will show your vision of this area in 2020:

— The first map will show population and land use.
— The second map will show the transportation and communication systems in the area.
— The third map will show resources management facilities for water, energy and waste disposal.

In addition, your group will be required to photograph a present day area of the watershed and then juxtapose that photo with a drawing of what you think the same area will look like in 2020.

This poster, along with the maps, will be presented and explained to the class during the last full week of school.

Remember: you are NOT starting with a "clean slate." You must note what currently exists in the watershed and forecast from there. This is, however, your chance to dream: to plan for the best possible future for our area, the place where your children may be growing up. What do you want for them?

APPENDIX G
Objectives and Outcomes

The following section lists the objectives and outcomes from the 1993 - 94 school year. The reader will note that many of the same concepts and even some specific activities remain from previous years.

WATERSHED
OBJECTIVES AND OUTCOMES
1993 - 1994

GENERAL

To fulfill the general requirements of the WATERSHED Program, the student will:

— organize and maintain a binder of all program materials

— maintain a portfolio of all written work to demonstrate progress in the process of writing, the use of various genres, and the ability to critique one's own work as well as that of others

— maintain a portfolio of all work in the visual arts, defend that portfolio with respect to the elements of composition, and be able to critique the work of others

— take (with a SLR camera), develop and print a successful black and white photograph

— complete a chapter for our class book which includes both written and visual elements in the appropriate forms

— complete all Tuesday Tasks and any other general assignments

— write folder comments and share the folder / work with parents each week

— create and complete projects above and beyond those assigned

— demonstrate effective use of materials

— demonstrate effective / productive use of time

— participate in all group activities such as discussions, games, reading sessions, SSR, and so forth.

SENSE OF PLACE

To understand the dynamics of a watershed, then student will:

— create a three-dimensional topographic map of a local watershed

— draw from memory a reasonably detailed and accurate map of our region and be able to locate important landmarks on it

— conduct a complete field study (with physical, chemical and biological parameters), then chart and interpret the results

— demonstrate an understanding of photosynthesis / respiration and the connections to systemic energy flows such as those in the human body, food chains and regional development

— demonstrate knowledge of water: its physical characteristics and its influences on all aspects of life such as living systems, weather, hydrology, and historical developments

— describe the characteristics of a stream (gradient, order, flow) and their connections to topography and ecosystems

— identify organisms found in and around local streams, and draw conclusions about their forms and ecological functions

— recognize and describe major regional rock types by characteristics, age, location, topographical significance and historical influences

— create a "Drip Essay" following the path of a drop of water along a stream and through the water cycle.

SENSE OF TIME

To appreciate the human interactions with watersheds over time, the student will:

— create an "American Diary" with ten chronological entries (listed), each demonstrating an understanding of a particular group of people who inhabited this region at different times;

- Lenape: Pre-Columbian culture
- Swedish Colonists (2): "The Voyage Over" and "The Letter Home"
- Miller's Apprentice circa 1710
- Quaker Life circa 1760
- Soldier at a local battle of the American Revolution
- Soldier's letter home from Valley Forge
- Powder Mill worker from Hagley / DuPont mills circa 1850
- 19th Century Immigrant's letter home
- Time Capsule letter to the Future circa 2020

— participate effectively in the planning and the presentation of group projects such as Lenape Feast Day, Create-a-Colony, and American Origins

— research a specified three year period of the 19th century, then create and present a newspaper (with articles, editorials, maps and illustrations) displaying the results of that research

— plan, conduct and present an oral history project covering an event or aspect of 20th century life.

SENSE OF QUALITY

To recognize the universality of systems and the impact of systems on the quality of life, the student will:

— research and create a facsimile of a painting by one of the Wyeths

— create a human body "map" showing the major organs and systems, and lead a "guided tour" of at least one system

— create a story describing a fantastic voyage through the human body

— produce and defend a hypothetical family budget which includes the expenses involved in buying or building a house

— design a home including scaled floor plans (with major systems), plot diagrams, elevations and a scale model

— produce and present a regional plan for this area in the year 2020 which demonstrates an understanding of regional systems such as energy distribution, waste treatment, water resources management, transportation and so forth.

The following bibliography is intended simply as a sample of the myriad publications available which lend support to various aspects of WATERSHED's whole learning philosophy and methodology.

Adler, Mortimer J. (1982).*The Paideia Proposal: An Educational Manifesto.* New York: Collier Books, Macmillan Publishing Co.

Adler, Mortimer J. (1984).*The Paideia Program: An Educational Syllabus.* New York: Collier Books, Macmillan Publishing Co.

Adler, Mortimer J. (1988). *Reforming Education: The Opening of the American Mind.* New York: Macmillan Publishing Co.

Barth, Roland S. (1990).*Improving Schools from Within.* San Francisco: Jossey-Bass Publishers, 1990.

Cetron, Marvin, and Margaret Gayle (1991). *Educational Renaissance: Our Schools at the Turn of the 21st Century.* New York: St. Marten's Press.

Dewey, John (1963). *Experience and Education.* New York: Collier Books, Macmillan Publishing Co.

Gatto, John Taylor (1992). *Dumbing Us Down: The Hidden Curriculum of Compulsory Schooling.* Philadelphia: New Society Publishers.

Glasser, William (1986). *Control Theory in the Classroom.* New York: Harper & Row.

Glasser, William (1992). *The Quality School: Managing Students Without Coercion,* 2nd ed. New York: HarperCollins Publishers.

Glasser, William (1993). *The Quality School Teacher.* New York: HarperCollins Publishers.

Howe, Harold, II (1993). *Thinking About Our Kids: An Agenda for American Education.* New York: The Free Press, Macmillan Co.

Kohl, Herbert R. (1969). *The Open Classroom: A Practical Guide to a New Way of Teaching.* New York: New York Review Books, Random House, Inc

Kohn, Alfie (1986). *No Contest: The Case Against Competition.* Boston: Houghton Mifflin, Co.

Lipsitz, Joan. (1984). *Successful Schools for Young Adolescents.* New Brunswick, N.J.: Transaction Books.

Martz, Larry (1992). *Making Schools Better.* New York: Times Books, Random House, Inc.

Neill, A.S. (1960). *Summerhill: A Radical Approach to Child Rearing.* New York: Hart Publishing Co.

Perkins, David (1992). *Smart Schools: From Training Memories to Educating Minds.* New York: The Free Press, Macmillan, Inc.

Sizer, Theodore R. (1984). *Horace's Compromise: The Dilemma of the American High School.* Boston: Houghton Mifflin Co.

Sizer, Theodore R. (1992). *Horace's School: Redesigning the American High School.* Boston: Houghton Mifflin Co.

Wigginton, Eliot (1985). *Sometimes A Shining Moment: The Foxfire Experience.* New York: Anchor Press, Doubleday, Inc.

Wirth, Arthur G. (1992). *Education and Work for the Year 2000: Choices We Face.* San Francisco: Jossey-Bass Publishers.

5088